Skylark Fields

A FORTIES CHILDHOOD

Alan Sheasby

Illustrations by Rosemary Booth

WARWICKSHIRE BOOKS

First published 1990 by Warwickshire Books on behalf of the Department of Libraries and Heritage of Warwickshire County Council.

ISBN 1 871942-04-7

Printed and bound in Great Britain by BPCC Wheatons Ltd, Exeter

WARWICKSHIRE BOOKS
Official publisher to Warwickshire County Council

An imprint of Wheaton Publishers Ltd
A member of the Maxwell Communication Corporation plc

Wheaton Publishers Ltd
Hennock Road, Exeter, Devon EX2 8RP
Tel: 0392 411131

Contents

Illustrations

Illustrations and Map

Rosemary Booth

INTRODUCTION

The North Warwickshire village of Caldecote, with its row of tiny terraced cottages, remains very much the same today as it was in the Nineteen Forties when the events forming this narrative took place. The drinking water tap, that we made such haste to reach in the several hot summers of the decade, has gone, but its red-brick surround can still be seen.

Unaltered also is the tree-lined road leading from Weddington to the Watling Street, which witnessed so many convoys of endlessly moving military vehicles and jeeps when the war in Europe began to turn in favour of the Allies.

The friendly Italian prisoners of war who marched along this road are probably grandfathers now, regaling their grandchildren with accounts of bitter English winters and of the curious children who were so fascinated by their round-patched prisoners' uniforms.

Sadly, the ten rival gardeners and Anderson Shelter erectors of Weddington are no longer here to read these pages. Most of their fiercely protected vegetable plots, which lay between poultry coop and pigsty, have been landscaped and lawned, with white plastic pots, holding forlorn looking geraniums, clinically arranged on patios.

The blue-grey roof tiles of the Parish Hall can still be seen from the gardens. Closer inspection could even reveal tiny blemishes where carefully aimed ball bearings found their mark during our delinquent period.

Signal Leys Gorse and the spinney containing the icehouse, apart from the loss of their elms, remain almost identical in appearance to that of almost half a century ago.

A testimony to the care shown by generations of Caldecote farmers.

No longer to be seen are the huge flocks of Lapwings, their soothing, unhurried flight being such a common sight in our childhood. Replacing them are hundreds of gulls; birds of cliff-tops and wild seas; an alien addition to our unassuming Midlands countryside.

The Ashby Railway Line, scene of several of our boyhood escapades, has been transformed by the local authority into a leisure walk. Each summer a remarkable variety of wild flowers mass together in colourful profusion, where once huge clanking steam locomotives thundered by, as we lay concealed on the embankment slopes.

Chapter 1

MY UNCLE SILAS

When I first encountered the literary delights of the 'Uncle Silas' stories, I must have subconsciously substituted my own father for the notoriously sly but likeable character so endearingly delineated by H E Bates. Although I cannot recall him having an ever ready supply of cowslip wine to imbibe from, as Uncle Silas had, he nevertheless possessed certain qualities which reminded me of the old rascal. A permanently youthful twinkle in his eye even when he was approaching eighty; a fund of reminiscences reliving his encounters with the Turks in Mesopotamia during the First World War; his travels bordering the River 'Uferatees' as part of the same campaign; and a love of the outdoor life in which gardening figured very prominently.

In the Nineteen Forties there was a rivalry amongst the gardeners of the ten neighbouring houses that comprised the Northern edge of Castle Road, which whilst never admitted existed none-the-less.

A wide variety of standards were to be found amongst the ten gardens. Some were non-descript, neglected and dull, while others appeared neat and well organised, producing encouraging results. My father's garden did not fit into either of these categories, being without exception the untidiest in the row, the footpaths rarely being swept. It was also the bearer of the most superb vegetables, soft fruit, apples and plums that you could conceivably imagine. These were all harvested not only by dint of hard work but also by his own secret, highly personal formula for home-made fertilisers.

The humid evening summer air above Castle Road was often overlaid by an obnoxious aroma, conducive to headaches, which provoked general mumblings of discontent from our immediate neighbours. Furtively mixing his concoctions on a flat square concrete repository, the magic potions were gradually perfected. He was never persuaded to divulge the secrets of these deadly mixtures, merely murmuring knowledgeably phrases that included 'sulphates of harmonia', 'nitrations' and 'boned meal'. But succeed they did, magnificently.

While my Uncle Silas was oblivious to his nauseous addition to the midsummer air, predictably, he was the first to criticise any of his fellow gardeners who had the temerity to light a fire containing organic material. All growing things were returned by him to the earth from whence they came, usually in the form of compost. Unwittingly, or otherwise, a neighbour, two doors removed, somehow contrived to produce slow-burning, densely smoking fires, that persisted for days on end. My father's usually gentle monotone would gradually increase in volume and his piercing gaze directed at the wretched fire and its perpetrator was wondrous to behold.

His onions, grown from 'sets', matured to become the size of grapefruit; his leeks possessed the girth of a man's arm; his Brussels sprouts resembled small green apples. Even in the driest summers his vegetable marrows were so huge it took considerable leverage to transfer them from marrow bed to kitchen. In times of water shortage I would wake in the stillness of night to hear the pleasant, sleep-inducing sound of running water flowing gently from the stopcock in our outhouse, to spread itself generously to a different part of the garden each evening. The flow mysteriously subsided at dawn leaving the garden lush and tropical; the neighbouring plots remaining parched, resembling dust-bowls.

My Uncle Silas never spoke of this miraculous aid to his gardening success, but the twinkle in his eye seemed to gain extra voltage.

Prior to dawn breaking in darkest January, an unearthly glow could be seen emerging from just beneath the surface of the soil in his tiny greenhouse. This eerie light was not a manifestation of occult forces, but merely the diffuse light of a hundred watt electric light bulb carefully covered with an inch of fine, fertile soil. To provide this unusual propagator, a cable had been fed from an electric socket in his small kitchen to emerge through its narrow window into a battered wooden shed, where, incongruously, his pith helmet had hung, gathering mould, for over twenty years. From there it found its subterranean way to the lean-to greenhouse where it protruded damply from the soil. This lethal looking contrivance, while defying all procedural electrical safety regulations, spread faint heat amongst the topsoil; enough to enable the minute seeds of polyanthus to germinate even though snow lay on the lawn outside.

My father's Anderson shelter, like the other nine in our row, consisted of several sheets of corrugated iron held together by sturdy nuts and bolts. It was gradually transformed into a chalet-style residence, bedecked with multi-coloured polyanthus in April, and with foxgloves in June. The shelter had been methodically fitted into a three foot deep excavation, and then covered with eighteen inches of soil to provide extra protection.

The flowers were there and so was the extra protection, and so also was a permanent deposit of still, dank water. It would have been approved by conservationists for it was home to several superbly healthy frogs, who once in the water were unable to leap out to freedom.

The other nine air-raid shelters in the row were erected flush to the garden surface, according to instructions, and appeared ugly and obtrusive when viewed in profile. But they remained dry, - and frogless.

Our immediate next door neighbour was a kindly, affable man who, like Uncle Silas, tended his plot with devotion and infinite patience. But, possibly because he was not in possession of the secret fertiliser formula was unable to produce the prize vegetable specimens appearing annually in my father's garden. While hoeing between his immaculately laid-out rows, our neighbour was able to pursue his other leisure time activity, that of an enthusiastic pipe-smoker. During the long summer evenings the pervasive but pleasant aroma of his St. Bruno fought hard against the deadly odour emitting from my father's compost area. His wife, like many God-fearing house proud ladies of that decade, banished him from the sanctuary of her immaculately tidy, clinically fresh living-room, to smoke out of doors. On many occasions the mature tobacco fumes from his pipe filtered through the dividing wall of his outside lavatory directly into ours, as we sat companionably side by side, separated only by the width of a line of porous house bricks.

* * *

In the days before the acronym 'DIY' became an integral part of the English language my father was a male pioneering champion equivalent of the ladies pursuit of 'make do, and mend'. One of his more notable achievements was to provide us with a soot-free chimney each autumn. This not only saved the expense of hiring the local chimney sweep but ensured that our winter coal-fires burned clear and bright.

The system worked well for many years. That is until he attempted his so called, 'fool-proof ritual', one autumn following a particularly cold summer after an unusually large number of coal-fires had been lit.

Cheerfully stuffing the black-leaded grate to the brim with oily rags, paraffin soaked newspapers, and a generous supply of creosote-matured kindling, he had confidently applied the match that would ensure another trouble-free winter of sparkling, smokeless fires. From that point things got a little out of hand.

The first indication that all was not as it should have been on that still, pre-dawn September morning, occurred when we were awakened by a thunderous, vibrating cacophony of sound. It passed by the internal chimney wall of our bedroom with such resonance that we assumed a Lancaster bomber was about to land on the roof. The situation provoked a case of 'panic stations' as, still muddled by our recent deep sleep, we were evacuated from the bedroom to assemble forlornly as a family group on the lawn at the rear of the house.

Pale-faced, agitated, and muttering, my Uncle Silas stared skywards with the rest of us as the external chimney stack gave vent to an eruption of Etnean proportions. Such was the pressure from the furnace of ignited soot that the billowing smoke and flames spurted not only from the chimney pot, but forced themselves from between minute gaps in the heat-shimmering mortar which had for years held the bricks of the stack together.

It was far too early in the morning for other residents of the street to be about their everyday affairs, so we prayed alone as the sky above Castle Road, (which by now should have been rosy in the east), gradually assumed a depressing hue as if storm clouds were imminent.

We somehow survived without having recourse to call-out the Fire Brigade, the internal walls of the house remaining cosy and warm for days afterwards.

As the fire miraculously subsided my father's jaunty step automatically returned, and afterwards, as he quite rightly remarked, such was the purge, we were able to dispense with the services of the chimney sweep for two successive winters.

* * *

Keeping Uncle Silas company in the late Forties was a Blue Roan Cocker Spaniel. The fact that his name was Kim owed little to Rudyard Kipling. There was never the remotest possibility of Kim being entered for dog shows as his proportions defied his pedigree in the form of long, ungainly hind legs, which contrasted sharply with his rather short, stumpy forelegs. Completely disobedient and feigning deafness on suitable occasions, he lived an active, adventurous life and died when he was just fourteen years of age.

My father arose at 5.30 am in both winter and summer; his first task being to let Kim escape from his sleeping quarters in the small, warm kitchen. Practising on the way, he galloped down the concrete garden path to the adjoining field where his completely pointless and infuriating barking successfully awoke all the sleeping residents in the houses on either side. He was never to grow out of this tiresome habit, which, while it was just acceptable on mellow summer mornings, provoked intense irritation when attempting to sleep through icy winter dawns.

Energetically scraping his paws against the turf, he would bark at most things that moved, but more particularly at cats, postmen, and refuse collectors. He was a terrifying sight, strutting stiff-legged, showing his teeth, but, as we all soon discovered, beneath this ferocious exterior lay the heart of a complete coward.

At frequent intervals he would fly headlong from garden to field in pursuit of his greatest enemy, the domestic cat. With flapping, wing-like ears and enormous hind legs kicking high he would disappear in seemingly triumphant pursuit. After an interval of perhaps a minute his hysterical barking would change in an instant to the high-pitched howl of defeat, and he would re-appear with the spitting, furious cat mere inches away from his tail, and gaining all the time.

In addition to being a coward he was also completely two-faced; devoted to his master when there was no one else to provide affection; becoming automatically disloyal when other humans joined the company.

Despite these imperfections he was a magnificent companion, particularly when exploring the woods and fields of Caldecote. Our excursions took place at least twice a week and frequently exceeded five miles of hard walking. Regardless of command he would invariably seek to show-off in water, where his agility and tremendous stamina were seen to good effect. During hard winters he would swim in streams which had iced banks, his long black ears spread out on the surface of the water. A covey of partridge was a familiar sight in the Forties, whirring away above the ploughed land, heading for the sanctuary of the next hedgerow. Kim was adept at sniffing them out. Similarly, he would put to flight long-legged sandy coloured hares; barking excitedly; losing ground from the start of the chase, but never once giving up.

Appreciating life's little comforts, he went missing from home for just one night in the whole span of his fourteen years. Because it was feared that he might be disturbing sheep near Anker Cottage, he was locked up for the night in a cold stable attached to the farm outhouses. He returned home the next morning chastened, his whole manner exceptionally subdued and dejected. Kim was never to leave home alone again.

Anker Cottage in 1955

Beneath his feigned aggression lay the gentlest heart. He never once bit anyone, it was all show. The only time his ferocity appeared to be genuine came in the aftermath of one of our annual pig-killing days. Shortly after the sides of pork had either been salted or roasted, he emerged from the cool, narrow pantry with a joint of roast pork so enormous he was able only to drag it over the red quarries. For once his anger at being deprived of it came straight from the heart.

Kim's footprints are still to be seen, embedded in the concrete of the garden path, which he used every day as the most direct route to his early morning barking pitch.

Chapter 2

YOUNG FARMERS

Set on Weddington Lane, approaching Caldecote, a mere half mile from where we lived, were two small farms. They were owned by brothers and the farms, in fact, adjoined each other. We knew them affectionately as 'Pop' and 'Uncle Tom', and while farmers in general were our sworn adversaries, both Pop and Uncle Tom always held our respect and indeed, admiration. They both appeared to be very old to us, but they were probably only in their fifties.

Pop ran a small milk-round with his pony and milk-float, serving fresh milk directly into decorative jugs with a ladle from his silver churn, while standing on our doorstep. He was paid for his services each Saturday, and, for no reason that I could discover, invariably gave to me a 'Saturday penny' when transactions were concluded.

As we approached our teens, four of us, from Castle Road and Church Lane, began to perform menial tasks on Pop's farm. We were taught how to milk, clumsily at first, but gradually acquiring the knack, eventually becoming reasonably proficient. Sweeping out cowsheds was unpopular, but when we were each handed a half-crown piece for our troubles we were truly elated. Pop's farm was somewhat larger than Uncle Tom's and included a considerable acreage of pasture land which provided hay in early summer. Hay-making was a regular, pleasant, but rather monotonous task for the four young farmers.

So much so that I can only recall in detail one afternoon, from the scores we participated in, mainly because of the exciting event with which it concluded.

On that day the abundant hay was piled particularly high on top of the wooden haycart, but in a rather loose and haphazard fashion. The cart was pulled by one of the two huge shire horses who were an essential part of the farm's working team. One of the chief rewards for the four young farmers was to return along Weddington Lane, to the farmyard, while seated precariously on top of the hay.

We were half way to base when the whole load gently, quietly, but inevitably, slid off the wagon and subsided on to the road beneath us. I was fortunate in that I experienced a perfect, smooth, even enjoyable landing, with no after effects, but one of my companions sustained a badly bruised leg and was also, rather frighteningly, buried beneath the fallen hay for several minutes. Traffic must have been present on the road at the time of the accident, but I do not recall it. Nor can I remember how the hay was cleared from the carriage way. It seems likely that my injured companion and myself made as hasty a retreat for home as was possible in the circumstances. My friend was unavoidably absent from school for some time after the events of that summer afternoon. However, he was nothing if not resilient for he, together with one other of the young farmers, became regular part-time workers on Pop's farm, only relinquishing it when the quest for greater financial reward proved to be a necessity.

* * *

The approach to Pop's farm consisted of a tree lined drive which was perhaps a quarter of a mile in extent. The drive was patrolled by a score of extremely free-range hens and one ferocious and particularly aggressive, crimson combed Rhode Island Red Cockerel. On several occasions we vaulted the brookside fence in an attempt to escape his wing flapping onslaughts. Passing through a herd of Friesians, consorting with a Hereford bull, was much less of a hazard to us than was this strutting, militant rooster.

We also treated with great respect the two hefty shires, one grey, one chestnut, who complemented the temperamental Fordson tractor as the farm's pulling power. In harness, and impressively, but quietly employed, they gave a false impression of docility and aloofness. But when we came across them unexpectedly in their feeding pasture, aggressive tendencies, we assumed they did not possess, would appear.

Weddington Walk Railway Bridge

Jules, the grey shire, invariably sighted us when we were a full field away. Then with raised head and ears pricked, he would thunder towards us in what we took to be an ill-tempered canter. We were too nimble, and full of the adrenaline of flight, to ever stay in the same field as Jules. Perhaps he was being friendly and looking for companionship; we did not wait to find out. By the time he reached the five bar gate we had disappeared on to the small branch railway embankment called the Ashby Line.

The Ashby Line was the scene of one of our more dangerous and foolhardy escapades. Positioned alongside the always deserted railway line, lying directly in the path of our regular excursions, was a small wooden hut. It was invariably left unlocked and proved far too much of a temptation for us not to explore within its cramped confines. Inside we found a considerable number of fog signals; small detonators with straps to attach them to the railway line. It was the easiest thing in the world to place several of them along the track at intervals of some fifty yards, and for us then to retire to the safety of the hedgerows, as an engine approached. What a cheap thrill we experienced when the calm of a tranquil day in mid-summer was shattered by the exploding fog signals.

Placing an old, blackened, King George V penny on the Ashby Line, before lying in wait to watch the steam engine pass over it, remained a simple, if expensive, pleasure. It is difficult now to recapture the thrill we experienced each time we recovered our wafer-thin, saucer-sized pennies, after a huge, clanking steam engine, together with assorted trucks had run over them.

Adjacent to the Ashby Line, approaching the Watling Street, was a fine natural pond. It was covered on two of its banks by hawthorn, bramble and alders, but had an open aspect at both its northern and southern ends. While there were minnows and newts to be caught, and frogspawn to be lifted from its faintly amber coloured waters, the pond's main attraction was that it proved to be ideal for sailing model yachts, and if they were not to be had, floating logs and branches from one end to the other.

Water always attracted us, and the rather cumbersome vessels that we sailed on the pond took on the roles of the cruisers Achilles, Ajax and Exeter, out to sink the Graf Spee in the battle of the River Plate. The battles that were so graphically described in the BBC news bulletins were enacted very seriously on our quiet pond, set in a peaceful Warwickshire field.

* * *

Returning home from the yachting pond, heading for Weddington Lane, we passed through a large undulating pasture. On windy, sunny, March days, the approach of fast moving clouds from the west provided us with another exhilarating diversion. As the dark shadows of the speeding clouds hurtled towards us from the edge of the field, we ran to meet them as fast as young, brown, scarred legs were able. When the cloud shadows enveloped us, we threw ourselves forward onto the springy turf in submission. A rather pointless pastime, but one that remains as a vivid memory, even though nearly half a century has elapsed.

On the edge of this field was a narrow, ever present stream. It was remarkable in that it refused to dry up in hot summers, nor did it flood in winter. We drank from it regularly without suffering any adverse after effects, but our main use for the stream was to prepare crudely constructed dams across its brief span. Our reward was to see the once clear, now muddy water, slowly build up against the wall of branches and miscellaneous stones, so that the level in front of the dam was a foot deeper than that immediately beyond it. By the time we had tired of this activity the pressure of the water had penetrated the dam, and carried most of the unnatural construction away downstream to eventually feed into the River Anker.

Reaching Weddington Lane, and walking towards Tom's farm, we frequently encountered a pair of playful short-horned bullocks who resided in the roadside pasture. They were extremely small in stature and appeared to genuinely welcome our attentions.

Gripping a horn in each fist we wrestled and pummelled the playful beasts who in turn sportingly co-operated with great gusto. The first few contests resulted in an honourable draw, but as the bullocks rapidly grew larger and more enthusiastic there came a day when we wisely declined to accept their regular invitation to test each other's strength.

* * *

Uncle Tom's farm was much smaller, more of a small-holding really. It was run from a terraced cottage, which was a field's walk away from a combined L-shaped barn and cowshed. Tom was a rather short, thick-set man, with a silvery walrus moustache and a gentle husky voice. He was infinitely patient and not once did he object to the presence of two small boys accompanying him, trespassing freely in his barn, and playing Cowboys and Indians around his haystacks.

Despite his placid nature we were never able to outwit him. One morning we discovered several hens eggs lying on the turf, well away from the poultry coops. We discretely re-located them to a new position in the field, fully intending to take them home with us when the time came. Our intentions were thwarted when Uncle Tom quietly enquired of us as to the whereabouts of the missing eggs; producing from us embarrassed attempts in a weak show of innocent surprise.

Immediately to the east of the barn and cowshed complex on Tom's farm lay a small pond, so densely surrounded by hawthorn and bramble that it remained successfully hidden from all but the most persistent explorers. It had but one tiny access point situated on its southern fringe, which necessitated scrambling down six feet of almost vertical, invariably muddy bank. Virtually all of the pond's surface was festooned with various forms of water weeds, while broken branches and twigs littered the remainder of the still, teak coloured water. It was a breeding place for flies and mosquitos, which zoomed just above countless water-boatmen. Occasionally Emperor Dragonflies, turquoise and green, with shimmering gauze wings, would dart past. There was only one weed-free area of the pond in which we were able to cast our floats, an operation made even more difficult by the presence of the thick hedge both above and behind us. We fished the pond on numerous summer afternoons, sustaining irritating insect attacks, but never once were we to catch the hoped-for roach, perch, or even a lurking pike.

However a great consolation prize was to be won from the pond by the novice fisherman, for on each cast our floats almost instantaneously dipped below the surface of the water. The pond was literally full of minnows and sticklebacks, large and small, and with no predators to decimate their numbers, they multiplied in great abundance. We reeled-in two, sometimes three, minnows at a time when using orthodox hooks, but even the usual standby of a bent pin produced immediate results.

Although we rapidly tired of this most successful form of angling, the first half an hour of each session was always a delight. We returned all the fish to the hidden pond, while their companions queued up to be caught; their shoals being seen quite clearly as they swam near the surface of the dark water.

It was often possible to see a Kingfisher flying rapidly, then gliding between the banks of the slow flowing River Anker, which was situated one mile away to the west, but we were never to record his presence at this feeding paradise.

* * *

Tom's small farm-house served a dual role. It was ideally situated for its main purpose, but a sign attached to its narrow front door proclaimed that it also sold cigarettes and mineral waters. By blatantly purchasing five Woodbines in flimsy paper packets, ostensibly for our fathers, we were able to indulge in the delights of smoking our first cigarettes.

The barn and the surrounds of Tom's other small pond that was rumoured to hold golden carp, proved safe hiding places to perform the sacred ritual. This experience did not deter us from the habit of smoking as we grew older; our main concern then was to chew obnoxious, strong tasting sweets, in an attempt to remove traces of tobacco odour, before daring to return home. However, we did take seriously the threat that smoking could retard your growth.

Bales of straw, priced at six-pence each, were also sold from the farm house, providing essential bedding for the poultry and pigs that so many of us kept. The short distance from the farm, along Church Lane to home, carrying this cumbersome load over undeveloped shoulders, was an uncomfortable experience, and one which we attempted to avoid if at all possible.

Tom's son worked on the smallholding and while possessing a more serious demeanour than his father, every so often would enchant us by producing the oldest, darkest brown, most mature cricket bat you could ever imagine. It was instant cricket. The pitch was the narrow footpath leading to the barn used by both humans and cows. Using this rutted track Tom's son bowled a succession of prodigious off-breaks that turned wickedly, proving quite unplayable. Despite this it was still enormous fun, and Tom junior was always fair in allowing us a reasonably long innings with his antique bat.

As we walked towards home from the farms, we occasionally made a detour in order to pass a small row of semi-detached houses which were situated alongside an undeveloped ash-covered path. A lady resident from one of the houses was invariably sweeping her drive as we passed by; her tuneful rendering of 'It's a lovely day tomorrow', echoes sweetly in the memory even now.

Chapter 3

STREET-WISE

The traditional street games that we played, with great enthusiasm, after school, and at weekends, in the Forties, (apart from conkers), did not appear to follow any seasonal pattern. There were whims and crazes for a particular favourite, which would run its course for a few weeks before enthusiasm waned, it then being replaced by a game which was often decidedly different.

One distinct advantage that the relatively traffic free roads provided, was that games such as marbles, (or 'alleys' as we called it), and French cricket, could be played on side roads with little risk of accident. In fact, French cricket, where the central player defended his legs from a tennis ball with a cricket bat, was always enacted in the middle of a side street.

The simple version of marbles frequently took place on our return journey from Higham Lane School. Attempting to score a direct hit on your opponent's marble was played the whole length of the roadside gutters. Naturally many prized, beautifully coloured glass alleys disappeared down drains which occurred every fifty yards or so. Ball-bearings, as substitute marbles were allowed without demur, but disputes arose as to possession when they were won under the accepted rules of the game. They were considered to be worth at least two or three of their glass counterparts.

Another well-loved variety of the game of marbles was where up to twenty were placed within the confines of a chalked circle. Two players took turns in an attempt to knock as many as possible out of the area from a set distance. Those removed were the victor's rightful spoils. However, owners of ball-bearings, which obviously had extra fire-power, always forced more out of the circle than did those with traditional glass 'alleys'. Arguments often ensued!

Collecting cigarette cards was a favourite pastime and complete sets were greatly prized. A popular game, using cigarette cards, was also regularly played in the middle of a side road. The two, or more, participants alternately 'flicked' a card with index and middle finger to spin and float to the road surface some six to ten feet away. The object was to land your own card so that it touched, or covered, one of those already lying on the rough gravel. If you succeeded you collected both cards.

A game of dexterity and no little skill.

The chalked layouts of Hopscotch appeared at regular intervals on the rectangular pavement slabs whenever the game came around in favour once more. A piece of broken roof tile was used to attempt to attain the required square. This was a game that was often played alone and, again, a considerable amount of skill was called for. Physical fitness was improved, and leg muscles hardened with the controlled hops and tight turns that were an integral part of the game.

A frequent pastime, which profited from quiet streets, took place when we gradually perfected the art of controlling an old steel bicycle wheel rim with a short stick, while running along side it at varying speeds. It became quite a noisy operation when several of us circled the small green outside the houses, using the stick to manoeuvre the rim around tight bends. Few complaints were received however, and while scarcely realising it, we were again improving stamina, and our powers of co-ordination.

As we grew older and fitter, the traditional game of Hide and Seek took on a much wider dimension. We progressed from hiding in the immediate vicinity of outhouses and garden sheds, to explore the further horizons of the surrounding fields and woods. A whole summer's evening could be devoted to just one game of Hide and Seek, commencing when the quarry loped steadily away to the flat countryside immediately to the north of our row of houses. It was not unusual for a game to be abandoned without a successful conclusion, as there was such a wide area in which to hide, and to search. For the quarry to return home some hours later without even contacting the group again that evening, was considered to be a victory, even if the process was a lonely one. A post-mortem would be held on the following morning, when the elusive prey would reveal the route he took, and whether or not he actually saw his pursuers.

* * *

There were three types of leisure activities that we followed slavishly, which could only be described as combative and, potentially, highly dangerous. Our bows and arrows, catapults, and swords were all home made, and lovingly and ingeniously constructed from the limited materials that were available to us. The legends and exciting events surrounding the life of Robin Hood were brought to life for us in the unlikely guise of Errol Flynn. He took the starring role in the film of Robin Hood's adventures, which appeared at one of our local cinemas towards the beginning of the decade. We did not aspire to dress in Lincoln Green but none-the-less our bows were made from the finest hedgerow saplings, and our arrows, straight and slim, cut from the centre of any suitable wayside bush. If twine was not available, the bow string was fashioned from 'War Economy' brown hued cord. A bow was considered to be satisfactory when it took a considerable effort to pull the taut string back the necessary few inches, without the bow itself losing its rigidity. Arrow-tips were weighted with either black adhesive tape, or occasionally, to make them really lethal, the steel head from a playing dart. Good fortune and our own skill helped to avoid any serious accidents. A practised operator with an efficient home-made bow, could propel a weighted arrow a distance of one hundred yards. Sad to say we often aimed at birds, and always missed, but it was a thrill to see a speeding arrow pass through a flight of starlings, and fall to earth a considerable distance away.

While patiently assembling bows and arrows, our home-made catapults also demanded some rudimentary skill in fashioning the fork and attaching the elastic to obtain the maximum amount of thrust. In fact, we were quite happy to pay a few pence to the one expert designer of these weapons whose reputation circulated, and was duly admired within the local schoolboy fraternity. Rough-hewn wooden forks graduated to smooth, shiny, steel as quality control began to improve. We used heavy duty, quarter of an inch square, grey-black elastic. This took a somewhat muscular, controlled, stiff armed pull in order to ease it back prior to propelling the missile. Smooth round pebbles proved to be ideal ammunition, but, when they were available we indulged ourselves with small ball-bearings. These, because of their aerodynamics, travelled much further, following a truer trajectory, towards the target.

Before setting out on our regular countryside excursions, the catapults were carefully concealed until we were well out of sight of built up areas. Regrettably anything that moved was considered fair game for a passing shot. Scarlet-faced moorhens frequenting the banks of the River Anker, were much more frequent in the 1940s than now; they also provided quite a large, slow moving target at which to aim. Fortunately, as with our bows and arrows, we were still unable to cause many casualties, even though there were numerous near misses.

However, one tragic event lingers in the mind. As we returned from a morning's expedition in the fields just east of Weddington Lane, I made a random pebble shot from the base of a then thriving elm tree. The pebble ricocheted from trunk to branch on its way skywards and, as its force was spent, a small floating leaf-like object descended gently to earth. It fell to our feet; a perfect blue and yellow titmouse; a tiny globule of blood showing on its head. We completed the journey home crestfallen and in preoccupied silence. The event was not forgotten, but it had served its purpose, for from that day we were never to shoot at wild birds again.

A potentially highly dangerous aspect of catapult shooting using ball-bearings was enacted when we lined up the blue-grey tiled roof of Weddington Parish Hall. The hall lay some one hundred and fifty yards from our back gardens in Castle Road. By careful use of angles and elevation, we propelled the ball from a fully stretched catapult and followed its flight until it disappeared from view. Great satisfaction was derived from hearing the missile bounce, then clatter down the tiles an endless few seconds later. No doubt we were extremely fortunate that this target exercise did not result in permanent injuries to the innocent residents of nearby Church Lane.

Street lamp bulbs and the porcelain fittings of telegraph poles were other tempting targets, while a bottle top bobbing its way down the River Anker was a must.

A street game slightly less lethal, but not without its anxious moments occurred with the advent of the sword fencing craze. This was motivated when a film called 'The Mark of Zorro', starring Tyrone Power, was shown locally at one of the town's six cinemas. Our home-made swords were wooden and crude, resembling sabres rather than foils. Combat was pursued enthusiastically with the free hand either settled on hip, or held at an angle parallel with the head in true Zorro fashion.

Victory over an opponent was claimed when the letter 'Z' was scrawled with a flourish over his chest using the sword tip.

*   *   *

We came to be close friends of the son of the tenants who kept the local pub, known affectionately as 'The Grove'. He made an appearance each holiday on his return from a private school education. This was sufficiently unusual in our neighbourhood for us to initially treat him with a certain amount of mistrust. It proved to be quite unfounded and over a period of years the landlord's son slotted well into our young group, becoming as tough and fearless as any of us. He entered into the spirit of all our street games with genuine enthusiasm.

As our friend's experience at boarding-school had given him a resilient, independent, and confident approach to life, we were rarely able to emerge victorious in any discussion relating to our own boyhood achievements.

Until one day, and completely out of the blue, we casually mentioned to him that we regularly attended tuition classes in tap-dancing. Any of our local contemporaries would have immediately hooted with derision at this fantasy, but, incredibly, he believed every word of it. From that moment we milked the situation for all we were worth. We would interrupt any of our normal street games to announce that it was imperative for us to practice 'Routine Number 3' in readiness for our next tap-dancing lesson. Then, whirling grotesquely, boots beating a tattoo on the road surface, we would launch into a bizarre and obscene parody of a Fred Astaire dance number.

His face, as he watched this ludicrous performance, invariably remained serious and attentive. He was genuinely impressed, as we desperately struggled to maintain our decorum.

* * *

In addition to the street games and country pursuits that we were devoted to in the Nineteen-Forties, the games of cricket and football were, of course, entered into with boundless enthusiasm. In due course several players of note emerged from our ranks to represent their home town in both sports.

Obtaining cricket equipment was always a problem, but in times of dire need we used our ingenuity to fashion an original cricket ball. By cutting circular lengths from an old cycle inner-tube, then stretching them, one by one, over a hard core, such as a round pebble or an old golf ball, we were able to build up a solid heavy ball. The problem was that it bounced unpredictably and at most peculiar angles, when pitched on a good length. While practising alone with such a ball, one of my left arm fast-medium deliveries flew at remarkable speed from our small front gate, (which served as wickets), and disappeared just as quickly through our next door neighbour's bay windows. The guilt and recrimination that followed ensured that the 'devil ball' was, in future, used only when surrounded by open fields. The incident was made worse when I was reminded that precisely the same thing had happened as I practised shot-putting with half a house brick a year earlier.

Chapter 4

THE SECRET OF ICEHOUSE SPINNEY

One of our customary walks, using official footpaths, took us past a strictly private wood positioned one hundred yards from the main drive leading to Caldecote Village. In late summer scores of cheerful white-rumped House Martins sped the length of the spinney, occasionally flying between the trees before returning to their regular flight-path. A prominent notice attached to a telegraph pole on the edge of the surrounding field, proclaimed 'Trespassers will be Prosecuted', a phrase that when very young we took to mean 'Executed'; assuming that the two words had an identical meaning.

Naturally a sign such as this was seen by us to be in the nature of a challenge, so that very occasionally, when strict prior reconnaissance revealed that farm workers were occupied elsewhere, we hopped over the fence and loped into the wood. When viewed from a distance the wood provided an impressive symmetrical shape, standing out particularly clearly against the bright northern skyline. It was not unduly large, its beech and lime trees interspersed with occasional oaks and horse chestnuts. But towards the centre it gradually shelved on either side to form a natural hollow. At the base of the hollow, covered by bramble and elder-bushes, we were somewhat surprised to find the remains of a brick built icehouse. It had been used to preserve meat and other perishable provisions from Caldecote Hall which could be seen clearly just two fields away to the east. While this was interesting enough in itself, we were quite happy to leave the wood, not knowing that the hollow would come to serve another purpose in the years that intervened before our next visit.

Caldecote Hall after the fire in 1955

It was indeed a considerable time before we were to enter the wood again and we were soon to discover that all was not as it appeared on its verdant looking, grass covered slopes. The once familiar hollow lay beneath us as did the outline of the icehouse, so we decided to race down the incline and head for the far side in competitive style.

Our young legs took us towards the base of the hollow at a fair speed, when to our horror we realised what was now stored there. In the intervening period since our last visit, layer after layer of slimy, green, cattle manure had been deposited in the hollow. This had gradually found its own level and blended into the surrounding surface of the wood.

On and on we ran, gradually sinking deeper and deeper into the foul sickly-sweet smelling bog. When it reached beyond our knees our momentum was spent, and, with considerable difficulty, we turned and extricated ourselves from the mire.

The return to the haven of the surrounding bank was accompanied by curses and great groans of distaste. Hilarity arrived a considerable time later, after we had scraped the outer layer of the clinging deposit from boots, stockings and thighs. Reeking from the pungent residue, and suitably crestfallen, we made our way home.

It was an experience we were never to repeat, nor did we ever reveal to anyone the hidden secret of Icehouse Spinney.

Chapter 5

WINTER 1947

The memories that remain from that frozen time over forty years ago contain nothing of the hardship and misery usually associated with a particularly hard winter. Quite the reverse.

We peered through small gaps in the living-room curtains out into the freezing night, where, lit by the room's reflection the snow fell interminably in a gentle, relentless swathe.

A silent prayer went up from small boys everywhere to please let it continue to snow - and snow!

We gave no thought to road conditions and the associated inconveniences that the blizzard had brought to adults. We saw only the pattern of falling snow against the single bulb of the street lamp, glistening as it silently feathered down. May it continue forever!

Ponds that during the previous summer had witnessed us hunting for newts, bullheads, minnows and moorhens nests, now became instant perfect slides.

One tree-lined pond that ran adjacent to Church Lane, avoided by us in summer as it appeared stagnant, containing unsavoury looking debris, was now miraculously transformed into a magical twenty yards of thick silver ice. A seemingly endless stream of oddly assorted boys and girls, queueing in orderly fashion it must be said, revelled in the delights of the slide.

No frayed tempers were in evidence, the only infrequent altercations piercing the freezing night occurred when participants were suspected of wearing boots with rubber soles, and were vehemently accused of helping to "chuck" the slide's surface.

During that hardest of winters, flood water seeped into the surrounding flat meadows from the sluggish, slow flowing River Anker.

Overnight the field was turned into a shallow ice covered lake. It seemed that we explored these fascinating frozen waters always at night, the moonlight from the clear freezing air being sufficient to guide our way.

Ice skates were unheard of, but with the aid of the universal brass-studded boots and shoes, we 'skated' on the surface of the flood with exhilaration and no little expertise.

During the day, fields and hedgerows were approached with some trepidation as they were so heavily laden with deep drifts of frozen snow. Even though they made our progress difficult, the thrill of finding the deepest drift was a reward in itself. Over the Wellington boot tops, past the knees, to the waist; snowdrifts to remember and compare scornfully with those of more mild winters. Chapped and sore legs above knee level were tolerated during the day, then treated each evening with 'Snowfire' ointment, guaranteed to soothe the chafed skin overnight.

Once an explosion shattered the icy morning air and we fled laughing from its source. Later we were informed on good authority that it had been caused by a tree branch reacting against the extreme conditions.

Chapter 6

OUTINGS

Those of us who were fortunate enough not only to live on the fringe of the countryside, but to be situated just one mile from the town centre were able to enjoy the advantages provided by both.

There were several seasonal countryside events which we followed year after year, anticipating them eagerly, and even as we grew older, remaining in thrall to them.

Simple events; collecting blackberries in September, conkers in October, and holly in December, were planned weeks ahead and looked forward to with a thrill of anticipation. To us, part of the inherent excitement was due to the fact that the best quality blackberries, the largest conkers, and the most abundantly berried holly trees were invariably to be found on private land. This gave that air of illegality which provided spice, and added to the pleasure of the outing.

Several favourite holly trees were available, for anyone interested enough, on the official footpath circuit surrounding Caldecote Village, a walk of perhaps four miles. We felt, as teenagers, that these particular trees were not worth considering as the clusters of berries were usually poor, and fell below our high standards. They were treated with disdain.

But forever etched in the memory is one dense monster of a holly tree. Each year it produced scarlet, waxen berries in such quantities that the tree's glossy, dark green leaves, so predominant in summer, were almost hidden by them. Positioned on the edge of a gloomy, forbidding, and decaying wood, it lay just beyond the village. It was also within sight of the Leathermills farmhouse, which was situated just one field away to the north.

The expedition party to collect the holly consisted of, at most, two boys, but quite often it was a solo outing. Mid-December, 3.00pm, on a dark weekday afternoon was the time to be in the vicinity of the tree.

Armed with secateurs, thick gloves and coarse string, the three mile walk from Weddington was completed to coincide with the arrival of a freezing, misty dusk. Half a mile away the farmhouse windows shone cheerfully. But cheerful or not, they seemed to contain a semblance of threat, even though we were never to be challenged. Ten feet up, in the centre of the grimy tree, lost from sight on our uncomfortable perch, our secateurs came into action swiftly and efficiently. Soon there was a layer of superbly berried holly lying at the base of the tree. After securing the string around the bulk of the unwieldy and prickly prize, we made our way home, experiencing a glow of euphoria and a sense of achievement.

Back at base, the holly was carefully laid out spray by spray, and, after tossing a coin for first choice, it was divided scrupulously and fairly; but only after considerable debate as to which branches contained the most abundant berries.

It was irrelevant to us in those far-off days, that the healthy light-reflecting leaves, together with the glowing berries would lose their sheen within a few days of being closeted in hot, airless living rooms.

The decaying wood and legendary holly tree were both felled some twenty years ago. In their place can be seen fields of oil seed rape, the vivid yellow expanse dazzling to the eye on sunny days.

* * *

Just two fields beyond the holly tree lay a patch of low scrub and bramble bushes. It covered, perhaps, an acre in extent, and we knew it as Leathermills Gorse. Each spring sweet scented violets were picked from its shaded banks. As the giant holly tree was prolific in its yearly supply of berries, so was Leathermills Gorse as generous with its crop of blackberries.

Even though the weather, in marked contrast to the holly trip, was autumnal and invariably hot, the blackberry outing was still tinged with the faintest breath of excitement. We relaxed only when the interior of the Gorse was obtained without confrontation, for the owner's farmhouse was situated on the actual edge of the wood, and we could see washing drying on a clothes line just over the hedge.

Quite often the blackberry outing was a family affair. Picnic baskets, which had been carried for almost four miles were soon emptied of their simple refreshments, and re-filled with fragrant, juicy blackberries, some of which were the size of loganberries. The gathering of the berries was always accompanied by the silvery autumnal song of robins. Red Admiral and Small Tortoiseshell butterflies settled on the brambles and threatening, hostile wasps flew too close for comfort.

For weeks afterwards we seemed to eat nothing else but blackberry jam. It was piled thickly onto rather grey, coarse bread, which had been coated with a thin layer of the somewhat rancid, hard, yellow 'Special Margarine' that substituted for butter during those years of austerity. At weekends, blackberry and Bramley apple pies helped to retain the spirit of the early autumn days, allowing us to reflect on the recent successful day spent in the mellow sunshine.

* * *

With the benefit of passing years, even the horse chestnut conkers appeared larger and more plentiful in the Forties.

The trees lining the road from Weddington to Caldecote, while providing a regular supply of conkers, could not compete with those to be found in an avenue of horse chestnuts through which we passed on the way to Lindley Airfield. A windy day just prior to the expedition was extremely useful in making the collection possible at ground level. But the element of competition and skill came when the best conkers were to be seen still attached to the most inaccessible and highest limbs of the trees. Fallen branches some two feet in length were utilised in a great show of strength and accuracy, in attempting to dislodge the prize conkers. It took many arm-aching throws to obtain a successful hit. Disintegrating shells together with bright shiny conkers, rattling through the branches before bouncing onto the hard grass surface, and occasionally heads, is an abiding memory.

Prior to playing the game of conkers the largest and most impressive nuts were gently roasted for a few hours in fireside ovens. Sad now to think of the impeccably satiny, smooth horse chestnuts so quickly reduced to dull, hard, misshapen competition conkers. It took some considerable pressure to insert a skewer when excavating the hole that received the knotted string. Great pride was taken in being the possessor of a champion conker, anything above a conker-tenner being a formidable adversary. Sharp practice was not unusual, the crafty teenager who lived next door eventually admitting to having injected a small amount of nearly set concrete into his champion thirty-oner.

* * *

We were fortunate in that ponds were still frequently to be seen in the Forties, often occupying corner sites of arable fields. While most of them contained only a selection of minnows and newts, together with resident moorhens, a few had the reputation of being the homes of monster carp and tench. Hours were spent patiently watching motionless floats in these permanently murky, cloudy textured waters, but rarely did they justify the legends.

Just beyond the avenue of horse chestnuts at Lindley was a large, attractive, tree-bordered stretch of water which became the object of another of our annual pilgrimages. The outing to Lindley pool stands out particularly clearly.

As on all the special days, planning and preparation had taken place a considerable time prior to the event. This was to be a fishing expedition and picnic combined, involving two family groups comprising mothers and an assortment of sons.

The myth that all the picnic days of youth were bathed in idyllic sunshine was abruptly destroyed. This particular one started with steady, relentless rain which continued on and on throughout the day. However, not for one moment was the spirit of the group deflated; the walk to the pool, some four miles, taking place in a mood of optimism and good humour.

On the sodden bank of the pool our fishing rods were carefully slotted together; lines, floats and shot prepared; bait attached, and the first casts made. The whole length of water was continuously pitted by the sweeping rain, which did not at any time show the remotest sign of easing. Apart from undulations caused by the rain, and the slight ripples of the pool surface, our floats remained absolutely stationary throughout the whole day. By early afternoon it was tacitly agreed that it would be better to accept that this was to be one of our least successful outings, and preparations were reluctantly made to return home through the deluge. At that moment, as if to give just a tiny reward for our perseverance, my brother lifted from the pool a small, but extremely lively, red and silver perch. Somehow this made the whole day worthwhile.

As we departed a pair of mallard flew from an old tree stump on the pool bank, leaving behind two large eggs in the tree's hollow base. My memory is hazy about the fate of the small perch, but I recollect that the duck eggs certainly accompanied our journey home.

On reaching home I was immediately despatched to bed even though it was only mid-afternoon. This was a most unusual occurrence, and was a well meaning attempt to forestall any possibility of a chill that our soaked state may have initiated. I was awakened a short time later feeling very refreshed and full of well being.

From that point the day improved considerably. Dry, fed, and with a change of clothes, the fishing expedition members met and walked the one and a half miles over Weddington meadows to the Ritz cinema. There, we were all entranced by Ronald Colman and Greer Garson who starred in the film "Random Harvest". A tear-jerker in the 'grand' tradition, but impeccably acted, it became one of my 'best half dozen films' in a boyhood of regular visits to the cinema.

* * *

Somehow, stealing apples, or 'scrumping', as it was always known, never once raised the faintest twinge of unease in our youthful consciences. Orchards and apples were fair game. They provided a challenge for us as we attempted to outwit the lawful owners, together with their defensive preparations.

An orchard attached to 'The Grove', the large local pub, was surrounded by a six feet high red-brick wall and was situated on the busy road that ran through Weddington. It was an achievement not only to scale the wall, (for we were only four feet something), but to do it unobserved, to find the tree filled sanctuary, away from the traffic, on the other side.

The apples from this particular orchard were nondescript and invariably sour, even though we were never particularly choosy.

By far the best apples were to be found behind a wire-fence on the edge of a private garden attached to a rambling, but dignified looking house, called rather grandly, 'The Grange'. The trees were very immature standing only five or six feet high. Fluttering narrow white labels attached to them revealed their pedigree. Each year they produced a small but luscious crop of bright red skinned Coxs' Orange Pippins, and the more green and tart-tasting Bramleys'.

The Grange at Caldecote as it is today

The mission to 'scrump' the Grange apples was planned meticulously beforehand, and took place after darkness had fallen on a mid-September evening. It entailed walking two miles, over admittedly familiar fields, after initially passing by the moonlit Weddington Church and graveyard. If even the slightest night sound had emanated from the vicinity of the graveyard, my companion and I would have instantly fled for home, although, naturally, this was never admitted. The shadowy fields and footpaths were so menacing when compared with their cheerful day-time appearance.

When the protective wire fence was reached, a period of time was spent listening for both human activity and prowling dogs; the bright lights of the large, isolated house shining only fifty yards away through the gardens. It took but a few moments to squeeze between the wires. Then with pulse-rates drastically increased, we procured as many apples as our pockets and rolled up pullovers would hold, before returning to the safety of the bordering field.

We were never caught.

It remains a remarkable fact that we ate nearly all the spoils on the triumphant journey home. Few were saved for the next day, for it would have been unthinkable to produce them in front of law abiding parents. Fortunately, healthy thirteen year old constitutions guaranteed us no permanent stomach problems.

These clandestine expeditions were a delight at the time, and it was only years afterwards, as our moral self-righteousness developed, that elements of doubt and guilt arose.

Well over forty years later two of the trees still remain. Bushy, overgrown and in need of pruning, they still produce golden and rosy apples each September.

Chapter 7

THE NEW SMALL-HOLDERS

The great majority of houses that were built in Weddington during the Twenties and Thirties, whether detached, semi or terraced, had enormous vegetable gardens attached to them. Most of the gardens were well tended and provided seasonal vegetables of high quality by dint of hard work and regular upkeep. 'Dig for Victory', was one of the phrases most commonly heard during the early years of the war, and with food rationing biting hard, many householders took the opportunity of utilising their surplus land and became minor small-holders.

Our immediate next door neighbour was the only gardener in Castle Road to follow instructions to the letter; he dug up his immaculate front lawn and sowed it with seed potatoes. It looked completely out of place, set against the adjoining flower borders and rockeries, and in fact the vegetables that were grown there never really prospered.

In all of our back gardens great activity was taking place, and soon most of the ten houses in the row saw poultry coops, rabbit hutches, and in at least two gardens, pig sties. In the quest for home produced meat, little thought was given initially to the developing attachment we soon felt for our rabbits and pigs. They soon came to mean much more to us than merely providing a supplement to our meagre rations.

Rabbits, black, white and brown, or a combination of all three colours, (but rarely the wild grey variety), provided the biggest problem. When they had grown to maturity, it became unthinkable that gentle Blanco and mischievous Loppy should meet a violent end just to satisfy our austerity ridden craving for fresh meat. And so they became permanent pets, completely defeating the object of their original purchase.

Loppy, a fine silky black doe with, naturally, enormous ears, had the capacity to escape from any box- wood, wire-meshed hutch, that we cared to build. For days on end she enjoyed her freedom, black ear tips occasionally being seen just above prized vegetables in gardens two doors away. Just as frequently as she escaped, so was she re-captured, with the minimum of fuss, showing little concern at her lost liberty and, once again, restricted confines. Such was her confidence in regaining her freedom just when it suited her.

* * *

Pigs were kept by only two householders in our row, chiefly because of the extra work involved, and also because of the difficulties that arose when attempting to obtain materials to construct a brick-built sty. Those of us who did venture into pig-keeping experienced the same moral dilemma induced by the potentially meat producing rabbits, - the pigs became pets.

Affectionate, greedy, and forever cheerful, our pigs were wonderfully resilient, intelligent animals, who soon came to know their regular feeding times. Forelegs splayed on the low brick walls, snouts, ears and wicked eyes peering over the top of the sty, they snorted and squealed their approval, anticipating the forthcoming feed. Gradually a rapport was established with their human keepers.

After months of intensive feeding the small pink youngsters were duly transformed into huge, bristly haired, immensely strong adults. Nearer and nearer came the day for the ritual of slaughter, and more and more withdrawn and anxious looking became the now attached ashen-faced owners.

Our local pig killer was a thin, elderly man with a mournful droopy moustache. Appropriately dressed in black, he cycled from Caldecote carrying his gruesome instruments in a large saddle hold-all. As soon as he appeared we hid our cowardly heads beneath blankets and eiderdown in an attempt to drown the frantic screaming of the doomed pigs, seemingly well aware of their impending fate.

Once the gorey ritual was over and the pigs bristles had been burned-off in a straw-filled fire, they became characterless impersonal sides of healthy looking pork. Any misgivings that we had experienced soon disappeared to be replaced by anticipation of the feasts to come. Large salted hams suspended from living-room picture- rails, replaced family group photographs and were admired far more than the pictures had been by visiting friends and relatives. So were the enormous joints of pork and the pies and chitterlings which followed. As there were few domestic refrigerators, the fresh meat was either salted down, sold, or consumed by the family and our relations as soon as possible. The unsalted joints were kept on a low stone thrall-slab in our cold, east facing pantry.

* * *

Poultry, invariably in the form of Rhode Island Reds, but occasionally interspersed with a few White Leghorns, was kept in the majority of the neighbouring ten back gardens, during, and just after the war years. The birds caused relatively few problems relating to their feeding and general upkeep; the whole project proving to be a tremendous bonus from the point of view of providing us with a constant supply of eggs and fresh meat.

Broody hens in small boxwood pens, sat behind wire mesh, on up to twenty fertilised eggs for what seemed an interminable length of time. Each evening the hens were allowed out to stretch their legs on the lawn, before quite happily returning to their restricted and devoted life. When the chicks were hatched, another fascinating chapter was witnessed in the neighbourhood's back yards. In addition to the revelation of actually seeing them extricate themselves from their shells, we mounted many life saving operations as soon as the more delicate fledglings showed signs of wilting. Trays containing sickly chicks were placed tenderly in fireside ovens where the gentle warmth revived what we assumed to be apparently hopeless cases.

As they developed into healthy young pullets and cockerels, we found a new and deeply satisfying pastime, which unfortunately caused some consternation amongst our elders. By impersonating their rivals in neighbouring gardens we were able to teach our cock birds the art of crowing. Soon, after a few initial rather distorted attempts, the whole neighbourhood was ringing resonantly with the clarion calls of the strutting young roosters. At the first signs of indignation from the now irate-looking adults, the smirking instigators melted quietly away.

One of the outcomes of keeping poultry and possessing a large vegetable garden was that the working man's gourmet-choice, egg and chips, became an almost daily meal. Potatoes lifted directly from the garden soil and eggs with shells still warm, enabled the poorest of us to quickly prepare a tasty and satisfying main meal. As this particular repast was invariably eaten accompanied by several rounds of stodgy, coarse grained, greyish, 'War Economy' bread, it remains somewhat incredible that indigestion was not considered to be a major health problem. To add to the potential of possible digestive ailments, our suppers consisted of a hunk of the aforementioned bread, eaten with a large piece of heavy-rinded soap-like cheddar cheese. It was also surprising that insomnia did not figure large in the discussion of common ills.

Chapter 8

BLITZ BOYS

There was no anxiety before retiring to bed, the imminence of regularly disturbed nights rarely being considered by small boys of seven or eight years. Then, vague realisation of being carried downstairs on dependable shoulders, bumping heads against the landing on the way, but too sleepy to be aware of pain.

To the Anderson Shelter; sheets of corrugated metal half buried in the garden earth, and then covered by another layer of soil. In daylight the shelter gradually moulded into the garden's surroundings, the topsoil providing vantage points for rosebay willowherb and foxgloves to tower in pink profusion.

Any consistent period of rain deposited a relentless level of six inches of dank water which seemingly never drained away.

Blanket covered benches in the shelter provided a minimum of comfort but no-one ever slept through the air-raid. The warning siren was heard only by adults; children in deep slumber would have slept on and on. But we certainly heard the 'all-clear', together with the heart felt cries of relief which came from the older occupants of the shelter.

The actual descent of high explosive bombs was more terrifying than the eventual explosion. The build-up began with the increasingly familiar intermittent throb of enemy aircraft, which were occasionally seen on clear moonlight nights. But it was the eventual release of the Heinkels' and Dorniers' bombs which provided the awesome, screaming crescendo of sound as they accelerated earthwards. This increased in intensity to culminate in the somewhat anti-climactic and almost comforting 'crump' of the actual explosion.

Incendiary bombs seemed, at the time, to be regarded almost as light relief. The nearest encounter with disaster that we experienced occurred when an incendiary glanced off the tiles of our sloping roof to the lawn below. The fearful message was relayed to us in the shelter, where we huddled together terrified in case the bomb would explode; but it was promptly and efficiently dealt with by the ever present bucket of sand.

When the bombing was at its heaviest during the Coventry Blitz of November 1940, the family would flee to the companionship of our immediate neighbour's shelter. This was almost certainly less safe than our own as it was erected without its covering of protective soil, and appeared somewhat stark and ugly set as it was in their pleasant garden. The brief, panic filled flight from one front gate then through the next was illuminated by orange skies which filled the Southern horizon over Coventry.

After the merciful 'all-clear' the sleep of relief followed instantly. But rarely was it an excuse to lie in bed when morning came. The morning after the raid was full of exciting options. If school was on the agenda, the walk to Higham Lane was made through numerous awesome craters which lined the road on either side. One in particular was of immense depth with toy like people standing in the dark red soil which lined the bottom. Popular comment was convinced that a parachute, or land-mine, had caused this devastation.

The air-raid shelter that had been built on the school playing field was a much more substantial building when compared with our own tiny Anderson Shelter. Steps at either end of the elongated brick built construction led down to its narrow oblong interior. Rows of benches and seats filled the gloomy internal space, but such was the general noise and excitement that never once was any semblance of enemy action ever noticed. The never ending repetition of, "Ten green bottles standing on the wall", filled the afternoon's interlude with a melancholy and monotonous familiarity.

The most civilised air-raid shelter, in my experience, was the cellar of my uncle's green grocery shop some five miles away over the Leicestershire border in Hinckley. It provided complete insulation from sound and the outside world. Neighbours, who were never allowed near the cellar during business hours, descended in some numbers to share reasonable comfort, together with the combined aromas of a grocery shop storage area.

It remains remarkable to me that the 'all-clear' was ever heard during the ever present calm and matter-of-fact conversation.

When night-time air-raids coincided with days off from school we experienced annoyance and frustration if we overslept and missed the initial hunt for shrapnel. With what possessiveness it was collected and hoarded! Small jagged pieces of steel with indecipherable numerals and letters etched into them were relatively common. Tail-fins and the solid grey detonators from incendiary bombs were star prizes and, surprisingly, were not all that infrequently found. It seemed that all thoughts of the danger associated with the bomb fragments had never existed, and the fearsome injuries that could have resulted from our coveted shrapnel were not contemplated, such arguments lost in the pride of possession.

As the years passed and the intense raids of 1940, 1941 and 1942 became an almost nostalgic memory, always good for reminiscence and companionable conversations, so did the bomb craters either gradually mould into the contours of the countryside, or became future sites for new housing and re-development.

Several small ponds appeared as a direct result of high explosive bombs, to become havens for moorhens, sticklebacks, newts and tadpoles. Sadly, they were eventually filled in and levelled, as farming became more intensive.

* * *

A daily sight on the main link roads during the war years was the long stream of service vehicles, Jeeps and gun carriers, known to us simply as 'Convoys'.

Using Weddington Lane, they filtered on to the Watling Street, the then main arterial road of central England, in a perpetually moving flow. Often a mile separated the first and last vehicle. As they passed we saw the vague, shadowy faces of drivers and personnel, and occasionally the perpetually chewing, always friendly American G.I.'s. Genuinely kindly, the oft-repeated phrase 'Got any gum chum?', more often than not received a generous response from our reluctant guests.

American army uniforms always appeared to us to be more comfortable and stylish than did their British counterparts. The material of their tunics and trousers tailored from smooth, expensive looking brown and fawn cloth, contrasted sharply with the coarse, hairy uniforms of British service-men.

The G.I.'s boots possessed a quality which gave impressions of comfort and ease in walking, with their thick pliable cushioned soles.

Our local branch of the Homeguard was, of course, much in evidence, regular Sunday morning exercises taking place in the nearby Weddington fields and meadows.

In the early days of the war wooden rifles were used by the earnest volunteers provoking many ribald comments from the curious onlookers. The sessions invariably ended at 'The Grove', the local pub, always depending on the availability of the supply of beer.

More involved, and serving a decidedly useful purpose to the blitz-weary residents, were the Special Constables, who patrolled the town during the heavy air-raids.

They showed remarkable resilience and stamina, many of them having been to work the previous day, re-commencing soon after the 'all clear' had sounded. The black material of the Specials' cloak-like tunic was home to the hardest, shiniest, teak truncheon it was possible to imagine. We secretly extracted, admired, and practiced with the truncheons before returning them to the voluminous interior pockets.

The Specials had their moment of glory when they took part in the great Victory Parade which wended its way through the town centre, marching proudly with hardened active service veterans.

From 1941 onwards, as eight-year-old children, we were subject to gentle propaganda in our daily classes at Higham Lane School. It appeared to work quite well. We were to avoid at all costs the 'Squander-Bug', and to put any surplus pennies into National Savings Certificates. We were also to collect as much waste paper as possible; this particular scheme incorporating a competitive element. To obtain the equivalent of fifty old books, or heavy periodicals, and have them recorded on the class list, meant that we succeeded to the rank of Captain. A small, coloured, cardboard medal was duly awarded to us, and this was worn proudly on our jacket lapels.

Gas masks were carried by all of us as soon as war was declared. We regarded them as unusual toys at first, and we tried them out for size and effect at regular intervals. Inevitably this diversion faded, and the masks and their cardboard containers became an encumbrance and an irritation to carry. Eventually they were used as weapons of combat as we swung the string-attached containers aggressively at our potential adversaries.

One unpleasant side-effect of wearing the rubberised gas mask was the internal build up of condensation around the facial area.

* * *

As the war progressed, small groups of Prisoners-of-War were seen more and more frequently both in town and countryside.

The German prisoners were generally aloof and serious-looking and rarely made contact with us, but the Italians, in stark contrast, tried to be friendly. Always willing to smile, their dark complexions and black greasy hair, together with their distinctive POW uniforms, ensured that they could be easily identified.

One Italian POW remains forever in the memory.

As we watched a small group of them marching along the road towards Caldecote, one of their ranks, somehow, surprised a hunting Heron from the marshy surface of a neighbouring copse. Clutching the distraught bird to his multi-coloured, round patched, prisoner's uniform he proceeded to strangle the wretched creature. Many boys in the neighbourhood possessed a good knowledge of the species of wild birds likely to be found in the area, but a Heron was considered to be something of a rarity. I remember we watched the incident in amazement. As there was no language contact we were unable to discover the eventual fate of the Heron.

While we were invariably advised by our parents to avoid all contact with strangers, this did not seem to apply to POW's, and I cannot recall any incidents to disprove this trust.

* * *

Above all these earth bound activities, ever present in daylight hours, Wellington bombers, Lysanders and Bristol Blenheims criss-crossed the sky.

Then Lancasters and Short-Stirlings become more and more evident, to be followed by huge Flying Fortresses when the Americans joined the Allies in Europe.

Chapter 9

PICNICS AND SUNDAY TEAS

It is perhaps a rather surprising fact that picnic teas were rarely embarked upon when we were boys. One of the reasons for their infrequency was the absence of luxury food, which makes eating out of doors such a pleasant novelty. Only one picnic outing stands out clearly. It took place during a summer holiday afternoon when our parents were out at work.

It was a somewhat spur of the moment idea formulated by two companions and myself. But enthusiasm soon took over, and we agreed to walk that afternoon to Signal Leys Gorse, and the pleasant river bank which lay alongside it. There we would consume our feast. This consisted of several thick slices, or doorsteps, as they were called, of outwardly crusty bread, but whose greyish, coarse interior texture, whilst making for healthy eating, did nothing to tempt our appetites. Hard, pale yellow, rather rancid 'Special Margarine' was spread as thinly as possible over the doorsteps. The luxury touch was provided by a liberal covering of apricot jam. This had been produced in Canada and arrived in the United Kingdom in large tins, not the familiar glass jars. The jam contained whole apricots and was delicious to eat on its own when we were not under parental observation.

As there were no biscuits or other sweet temptations, the hefty jam sandwiches were carefully wrapped in several pages of an old Daily Express, having first of all ensured that the latest episode of Rupert Bear had been read.

The River Anker near Signal Leys in 1955

With every attempt to control our will power, and showing great self discipline we set off on our post-lunch ramble to the wood where the brown water of the river ambled alongside. After walking for just half a mile the oldest boy in our trio succeeded in catching with his hands a large bullhead fish from the shallow, pleasant stream that lay just north of the Ashby Railway Line. Having no receptacle in which to place the pathetic, now gasping creature, he ran all the way home to Castle Road clutching the bullhead to his sodden jersey. He took no further part in the picnic outing; the fate of the bullhead remaining a mystery.

Another mile and a half of pleasant walking and we reached the picnic site. But somehow, during the ramble the last vestiges of control had crumbled away and frustratingly all that remained of the apricot jam sandwiches were several sheets of greasy, blackened newsprint.

On the rather downcast return to home, we somewhat sheepishly agreed that it had been foolish to expect two growing lads to walk several miles while carrying such delicacies.

Picnics were abandoned by us from that day forward.

* * *

Sunday afternoon teas however, were an entirely different matter. Having an aunt and uncle who were proprietors of a grocers shop, and who appeared to derive some pleasure from visiting their nephews, helped to make Sunday afternoons rather special.

We were able to tolerate, with a great show of patience, the interminable and, to us, deadly dull conversation that took place as a prelude to the tea itself. The talk revolved around the latest news of the Allies progress in Europe, ration books, clothing coupons and the general austerity which prevailed everywhere. Then came the ritual inspection of the long narrow vegetable garden. This entailed a detailed discussion covering each variety grown there; a serious and protracted business.

Patience was eventually rewarded when all six of us sat down to a carefully prepared table. This had been covered with an embroidered linen table cloth handed down to the family through the agency of a great-aunt, who had been not only thrifty, but remained independent of all help into her eighties.

A small tin of salmon divided into six minute portions was the initial appetiser. This was a great luxury during the war years, and was eaten together with numerous slices of bread that had been spread with blended butter and margarine. To follow, came home-made cake; a lightish coloured, rather coarse mixture of flour, powdered-eggs and margarine, interspersed with a few sultanas.

But there, in the centre of the table, on a three tiered cake stand, were placed the ultimate attractions; a selection of biscuits, plain and chocolate, with at least two wrapped in brightly coloured, luminous silver foil.

My uncle, who obviously remembered being a lad himself many years previously, always ensured that the younger members of the family had first choice. Our eyes never wavered from the shiny silver centre-pieces.

Only one feature of those memorable Sunday teas remains as a persistent, uneasy echo. While all the adults, who sat shoulder to shoulder around the small oblong table, seemingly delighted in eating the Caraway seed cake, which was always an integral part of the tea; to me, who possessed a permanently voracious appetite, it was akin to a nightmare.

As it was unheard of to refuse such a delicacy when it was politely offered around, my only object was to eat as little as possible of the sickly, perfume-tasting confection, and to attempt to swallow it without chewing or choking.

The apprehension that the Sunday Caraway seed cake provoked remains with me to this day.

While my aunt and uncle had the treasure trove of the grocery shop at their disposal, most households without this advantage nevertheless attempted to maintain some form of emergency store cupboard. The better stocked ones were shown off to visitors at every opportunity, and with no little pride. I can recall inspecting the neatly stacked cupboard of a family friend, which contained a remarkable variety of tinned meats and fruit, standing next to condensed milk and preserves. This cupboard was the object not so much of envy, as of wonder to us all, and futile attempts were made to emulate it.

Chapter 10

OF SPINNEYS AND FIELDS

The air-raids that took place between 1940 and 1942, and which caused such destruction amongst the houses lining Weddington Road inevitably provided ready made sites for the post war re-building programme. An unfortunate side effect prior to building the new homes was the necessary felling and levelling of several mature, narrow spinneys that grew parallel with the roads.

One of these small, rather nondescript strips of woodland was situated between Castle Road and Church Lane. It proved to be a colourful sight in early Spring, the grassy humps coated with celandines and delicate wood anemones. The rough pasture adjacent to it was home to Skylarks for six months of the year. They would arise in hovering song on fine days from January onwards.

Only once was I fortunate enough to find a Skylark's nest in this field. It was concealed in a rough tussock of grass and contained four earth coloured eggs. Visually marking the site as accurately as I could, I was still unable to locate it when I returned some time later, accompanied by a friend, who, of course, expressed silent disbelief as I grew more and more exasperated.

Immediately to the west of the Parish Hall was another narrow stretch of woodland which ran along Church Lane, near to the old Rectory and its walled gardens. A small stagnant pool that, when frozen, was our superb slide in the winter of 1947, gave way to an undulating path through the trees. It was hilarious to cycle on this switchback trail, particularly with two up on one bike.

Scots pines, together with stumps of dead trees, and low dense brambles, proved a haven for a variety of bird life. Spotted Flycatchers, one delaying its southerly journey until as late as October, regularly utilised the protruding dead branches to launch their sallies after insects. In late summer, polished blue, dark-red-faced swallows would rest for a while on these convenient perches.

During one spring a pair of Cuckoos haunted the spinney, flying to and fro, calling endlessly for several days in succession.

A narrow foot-path led from Castle Road, through the Skylark field, to the back gardens of the houses in Church Lane. It was a convenient short-cut to a friend's house, first passing through his long vegetable garden, where frequently to be seen were freshly killed cockerels, heads hanging downwards, slowly dripping blood. A gruesome sight! Nearer the back door, suspended from tree branches, soggy white muslin bags containing home-made cheese hardened in the prevailing westerly breeze.

This pasture, apart from encouraging our growing interest in natural history, was also the venue for several seasonal events.

A cricket pitch was cut and rolled each summer, and playing on this not unreasonable wicket was where we were to discover our life-long love of the game. In turns we were Denis Compton, Bill Edrich, Alec Bedser or Ray Lindwall. We imitated the erratic run up to the wicket of D.V.P. (Doug) Wright, and emulated the dexterity of Godfrey Evans behind the stumps.

On occasions we were fortunate enough to bowl with a 'corky', or orthodox leather cricket ball. This was invariably blackish in colour with thread protruding from its broken seams. A three spring Cannon cricket bat was a luxury, but more often than not we had to use extremely low standard, heavy pieces of substitute willow, which jarred the hands painfully when the ball was not middled correctly.

A lofted cover-drive into the hawthorn hedge on the far side of Weddington Road not only counted as six runs, but usually resulted in the ball being lost and play abandoned for the day. Only one or two boys in the neighbourhood were fortunate enough to own a cricket bat, a leather ball, and, in one case, a pair of yellowing pads. Naturally, they were always made most welcome to participate in our games. If, during the course of his innings, the owner of the cricket equipment disputed a dubious decision, he was invariably allowed to continue to bat. This prevented him from returning home with his gear, thus terminating our own game.

The footpath end of the cricket pitch was also the site for our annual bonfire. As soon as October came around again youthful memories conveniently forgot the hazards of a cricket ball lifting from a good length, and preparations urgently got under way for November 5th. The bonfires that we built on the cricket pitch were invariably huge; there being no shortage of fallen branches lying in the surrounding fields. In October 1945 to celebrate the Allies victory in Europe and Asia we made a sortie to Caldecote in order to collect several large branches from a fallen ash tree. Tying them together, we attached the loose end of the rope to the rear fork of the BSA motorcycle that one of our older brothers proudly possessed. When he cautiously accelerated away towing his unlawful load, we followed 'whooping' in the rear, small twigs and branches leaving an untidy residue on the road's surface. The larger branches swept from side to side as if they had a life of their own, as they were dragged at speeds approaching fifteen miles an hour towards the bonfire site. Remarkably this escapade passed without accident.

Fireworks were, of course, difficult to obtain, but somehow, my uncle at Hinckley, (he of the corner shop), always managed to procure a splendid box of Brocks assorted Thunderflashes, Roman Candles and Catherine Wheels, which complemented the Bengal Matches and Sparklers that most of us were able to purchase. Great emphasis was placed on the provision of a large quantity of food, as many neighbours turned out to share the delights of the enormous fire. Parkin, a traditional bonfire delicacy, made from oatmeal and treacle, was there for all to taste, but the main appetite appeaser was inevitably the plentiful quantity of potatoes, baked and blackened in the glowing ashes of the subsiding bonfire.

Such was the size of the fire that it smoked for days afterwards, as we constantly poked and prodded it, attempting to recapture the excitement of the night itself.

In this all-purpose field we played football, practising in-swinging corner kicks to imaginary goal posts, where a diminutive goalkeeper attempted to tip the ball over a nonexistent bar.

Home made high jump posts and cross bar were erected in the rough pasture, and we would spend hours gradually improving our performance, becoming elated when the bar was raised to a higher notch. The technique for high jumping in those days was strictly a scissors type leap from a narrow angle, the 'Fosbury flop' not appearing until the Mexico City Olympics of 1968.

A field game that never failed to fascinate us was realised when we connected two lidless soup tins with a length of string or cord some twenty or thirty feet long. As the string was drawn taut it was possible to speak into one tin to your companion, with his ear to the receiving tin, hidden in the grass some distance away. With only our heads visible we would advance on our imaginary enemy, relaying messages to each other through the seemingly magical telephone apparatus.

The rough, tussocky field at Weddington that bore witness to all these activities throughout the Forties, and which provokes so many nostalgic memories, was inevitably transformed into a housing complex. Skylarks no longer arise in exuberant song, and Spotted Flycatchers have no vantage points from which to pursue their prey. But the vociferous colony of Swifts still returns each May to the skies above Castle Road and Church Lane, as they always did.

Chapter 11

CANOES AND CURLEWS

In the late Forties our local milk-round, which had previously operated from Pop's farm on Weddington Lane, was taken over by a small, independent, father and son combination. The service, while perhaps lacking the timeless quality of the old door-step ladle informality, was, never the less, efficient, and probably more in keeping with the progressive times.

I gradually came to know the new milkman's son through his daily visits to the house, and quite soon, in regular conversation, I came to realise that his knowledge of the local wild-life was far and away in advance of my own. He spoke of Sparrow-hawk nests in the same way that I may have mentioned a Blue-tit's.

Without once appearing immodest, it became clear that his interest in ornithology encompassed a much wider dimension than did my own. This was not only due to the diverse number of species he was conversant with, but also because he had the means to travel much further afield in pursuit of his hobby.

In 1949 there was a considerable laxity in fulfilling the law relating to the collection of the eggs of wild birds.

Gradually, over a period of some months, the milkman's son confided to me that his own egg collection was his burning pride and joy. When, eventually, I was invited to his home to inspect his exhibits I was staggered to see not just one egg relating to each of the birds we had discussed, but whole clutches. They had been professionally presented in cotton wool lined drawers and labelled precisely as to their contents.

As it must have been very evident to him how impressed I was by this magnificent collection, he suggested that I might possibly wish to accompany him on his next bird watching expedition. Without waiting to be informed as to the object of the outing I gave an enthusiastic affirmative.

And so, some weeks later, on a warm May evening, we set off in his Rover to cross the County border into Leicestershire. Securely roped to the trailer behind the car was a magnificent lightweight bamboo canoe. It was perhaps twelve feet long and it contained two double-ended paddles. The canoe was regularly used by him to explore the Ashby Canal, which wound its peaceful way through Shenton and the Market Bosworth district.

Blissfully I sat in the passenger seat willing the evening's adventures to unfold. I was briefed that three separate enterprises were on the agenda for that pleasant late spring evening. As this was a much more systematic approach to the pursuit of natural history when compared to my own casual rambles around the well-worn Caldecote circuit, I was understandably impressed.

Taking a left hand turn from the Fen Lanes to the village of Shenton, I was somewhat surprised when the car came to a halt in the centre of the tiny complex of cottages. We walked over the bridge to the pleasant low-lying stream which bisects the village and there, following my friend's lead, we waited until all signs of human activity had ceased to be visible. When rural calm had descended all around us, and without wasting a second, he walked without hesitation to a thick trunked pollarded willow that nestled on the stream's grass banks. Concealed behind a layer of loose bark on the willow was a Treecreeper's nest containing four minute, whitish, redspeckled eggs. It took but a moment for him to transfer them all to his small padded collection box, and from there for us to beat a hasty retreat to the Rover.

Still captivated by his single-mindedness I was nevertheless, becoming a mite uneasy about the ethics of this type of wholesale pillage. Country lore, which had been instilled in us during our childhood, insisted that one egg only should be taken from a clutch, never more than that. Naturally, I was too much in awe of this professional egg collector to ever have dreamed of voicing my disquiet.

Leaving Shenton we motored on through the quiet Leicestershire lanes until we again deliberately, and I thought furtively, halted alongside a large hedge-lined pasture directly opposite Ambion Wood. His face a picture of concentration, he asked me, in hushed tones, to focus my binoculars to take in the further edge of the field, which lay perhaps two hundred yards away. Mystified, because my own efficient eyesight was unable to detect any signs of movement in that area, I nevertheless did as I was instructed. And there, walking unconcernedly amongst the grass tussocks, their long curved beaks probing the turf, I saw my first Curlews.

Passage migrants, birds of uplands and estuaries, my well-worn textbooks had always informed me; and yet here they were, in the centre of England, inspecting a nesting site.

To simply observe them in that pleasant location was sufficiently satisfying as far as I was concerned. Consequently I was more than a little relieved when my companion made no attempt to pin-point their nest as a preliminary to relieving the Curlews of their eggs. Perhaps my face had betrayed my inner feelings when the Treecreeper's nest had been ransacked just thirty minutes previously.

Still entranced with the evening's events, we progressed a little further between the hawthorn blossom bedecked hedgerows until we reached a point where the Ashby Canal became easily accessible from the road.

The sleek, narrow canoe was unloaded and carried lovingly to the canal edge where it was expertly launched. My friend, with great dexterity, seated himself on the tiny bench seat positioned in the bow of the craft, and I nervously followed suit in the stern. Gradually acquiring the knack of paddling, and just about managing to keep the canoe on a straight course, we edged forward almost silently beneath the tranquil evening sky. Panicking Moorhens and Coots frequently splashed away on either side of the advancing boat as we gained more confidence. Quite soon the streamlined canoe was cutting through the brown water at some speed. It was exhilarating, to say the least, and I spent the next few minutes rapidly formulating my own plans on how to become the owner of such a craft.

After perhaps half a mile of tow-path had sped by, my companion suggested, over his shoulder, that we should attempt to stand up in the canoe and continue paddling in the style of the Red Indians we saw so frequently at our local cinemas. This was easier said than done, but after a while we began to get the hang of the new technique, and our confidence and exhilaration grew with every paddle stroke.

Over confidence, unfortunately, for without any prior warning the Red Indian canoe suddenly turned through one hundred and eighty degrees, and we were pitched headlong into the reed strewn, cloudy water. Using the upturned canoe as a life-raft we struggled to the bank through the deceptively icy water. The evening's euphoria completely dispersed, we hid the now treacherous boat amongst the prolific massed ranks of cow parsley which lined the canal side, and trudged, squelching, back along the seemingly endless tow-path to the Rover.

Dripping water onto the leather seats, and feeling decidedly uncomfortable, we made our disconsolate way home.

After we had dried out, and obtained a change of clothing, the mood changed quite quickly from one of consternation to that of hilarity.

As the milkman's son continued to pay his daily visits to me, we were to recapture the events of that evening many times over the subsequent years.

We always exchanged news of bird sightings, but never of nests and eggs.

Chapter 12

FILM FUN, RADIO TIMES

We lived but one and a half miles from the centre of a small North Warwickshire town. It boasted six cinemas, which were spaced at regular intervals along its two main streets. They have all long ceased to exist being replaced by retail stores, entertainment halls and Bingo palaces, and in two cases having disappeared altogether.

During the Forties our visits to the cinema, always depending on available funds, took place at least once a week. Cinema going was so popular that queues assembled outside all of them each evening, regardless of what was showing. Queueing had become a way of life, and patience and tolerance were very much in evidence.

When an 'A' film was presented, those of us who were unaccompanied by our parents, frequently persuaded any reasonably respectable looking adult to take us in with them. A dubious occupation, both then and now. Safely inside, we found our own seats in the stalls set just below the permanent clouds of grey-blue cigarette smoke, which arose through the flickering projection lights. Immense, golden, illuminated silk curtains swept aside, layer after layer, before each film appeared. Not only were we patient when queueing, we were also rarely critical in our post-mortems of the films we saw. The great majority of them were filmed in black and white, but those in Technicolour were outright winners from the start.

Gene Autry and his horse Champion, together with Hopalong Cassidy, were our cowboy heroes, even if we did object to the musical interlude, set around the camp-fire, that seemed to take place in all of them. But our favourite Western star, by a mile, was the shadowy, magical Buck Jones, who featured at Saturday morning matinees week after week. He appeared in second feature western serials such as 'Riders of Death Valley' and 'The Phantom Rider'.

The other stars who we unashamedly worshipped, were Sabu, and Johnny Weissmuller. Sabu as 'Mowgli' in 'The Jungle Book', and as the star of 'Elephant Boy', and 'The Thief of Baghdad', stayed in our memories when other routine adventures were long forgotten. The Johnny Weissmuller, Tarzan films were even more exciting. We imitated his jungle calls with great enthusiasm when walking home from the cinema, reliving each moment of his tree-swinging adventures with Cheetah, Jane and Boy. He was always given an opportunity to show off his five-gold-medal Olympic standard swimming, usually as an excuse to rescue friend or foe in the statutory crocodile scene. Lex Barker, and all the subsequent Tarzans failed to inspire in us the type of admiration we reserved for Weissmuller. Even so, we were more than happy to see all the Tarzan films containing his successors.

Sitting through the films 'Beau Geste', and 'The Four Feathers', in a mesmerised state we entered a phase where we desperately wished to be youthful volunteers to the French Foreign Legion.

Gary Cooper as Beau Geste had a profound effect upon us. His desert adventures in conflict not only with the raiding infidels, but also with his brutal Sergeant, kept us entranced during the film and for a considerable period afterwards.

The adventures of Harry Faversham in 'The Four Feathers' exploited our pride in the then extensive British Empire, while at the same time providing a stirring desert drama.

But if we found these adventure films thrilling, our greatest enjoyment was derived from the many comedy films which circulated quite frequently to the six cinemas. The Marx Brothers' humour proved to be a little too refined for our juvenile tastes, but Abbot and Costello, George Formby and Laurel and Hardy pitched their performances exactly right, often leaving us breathless with laughter. Even more hilarious, and our number one favourites were, The Three Stooges. They appeared in short slapstick comedies usually as a support to the main feature. We were frequently in danger of making ourselves ill, such was our uncontrollable mirth. Fortunately for us, the whole cinema audience unashamedly gave vent to the relief of a great outburst of high good humour.

Of the other films that we saw during the war years several proved their eventual fame by becoming generally accepted as classics.

Ronald Colman in 'Random Harvest' and 'Lost Horizon', proved himself to be a fine sensitive actor, who never failed in his ability to induce tears amongst even the most blasé of his young admirers.

We sat through 'Gone with the Wind', without stirring for three and a half hours. Lifted by the emotional 'Tara's Theme', we were enthralled with the interplay between Vivien Leigh and Clark Gable, and captivated by the sincerity of Olivia De Havilland and Leslie Howard.

Walt Disney's feature length cartoon films were, of course, an absolute must, and while we adored Pinocchio, Dumbo and Bambi, the film which impressed us most of all was Snow White.

As seven and eight year old children, we found several of the scenes in Snow White to be genuinely frightening and disturbing. Not only was the Witch something of a nightmare figure, but when coupled with the scene where the forest trees turned into human form, with grasping branches clutching at the fleeing Snow White, we found it all too much to bear. Subsiding in tears, we averted our eyes from the screen.

* * *

It is difficult to comprehend how our morale would have fared in the bleak war years, and late Nineteen Forties, without the therapeutic and friendly accompaniment of the diverse 'wireless' programmes of that time. We came to depend on them not only for daily news of the progress of the war, but for dearly loved evening programmes that were warmly anticipated.

The Children's Hour programme that greeted us each weekday afternoon on our return from school, still provokes nostalgic memories of firm favourites; one in particular being Toy Town. S G Hulme-Beaman's stories proved to be the most popular of all Children's Hour series; its signature tune, 'Parade of the Tin Soldiers', introducing us to Denis the Dachshund, Mr Growser, Ernest the Policeman and, of course, Derek McCulloch as Larry the Lamb.

Occasionally as an alternative to saying 'Goodnight children everywhere', Uncle Mac's stand-in would sign off with, what we assumed to be, a special coded message, "Goodnight Chewall". It took several years to decipher that particular one.

G Bramwell Evens, better known as Romany of the BBC, and his spaniel dog Raq kept us entranced with their adventures in the English countryside. These reconstructed country walks were translated into book form; the annual volume becoming a regular gift at Christmas.

'Monday night at Eight' was a magazine programme designed for adults. It soon became equally popular with children. The invitation, enticingly put to music by Charles Shadwell and the Variety Orchestra, began, 'Its

Monday night at eight o'clock; Oh can't you hear the chimes'; and requested us to settle by the fireside with our Radio Times.

Our favourite sections of 'Monday night at Eight' were Ronnie Waldron's 'Puzzle Corner', in which we had to guess the deliberate mistake, and Ernest Dudley's 'Meet Dr Morelle', a thriller series.

Superior drama was provided by 'Saturday Night Theatre', which when broadcast at 9.35 pm proved to be a little too late in the evening for the youngest of us. Because his name was so easily remembered, it seemed to us that Howard Marion Crawford was involved at some stage in every performance. We particularly looked forward to Dorothy L Sayers' 'Lord Peter Wimsey' stories, which were broadcast in 1943.

Genuinely frightening and chillingly introduced in sepulchral tones by Valentine Dyall as the 'Man in Black', was 'Appointment with Fear'. The series dramatised stories by Edgar Alan Poe, and other thriller writers to great effect.

No one, in my experience, ever listened to 'Appointment with Fear' when alone in the house.

From 1946 onwards most of the houses in our street reverberated each evening at 6.45 pm to the sound of the 'Devils Galop'. This compulsive piece of music introduced us to the adventures of 'Dick Barton, Special Agent'. Noel Johnson as the first Dick Barton, with his intrepid colleagues Snowey and Jock helped the series to become a cult programme for all ages. When Noel Johnson was replaced by Duncan Carse and a succession of others, the adventures began to lose their hold on us.

A stirring signature tune entitled 'Coronation Scot' heralded another of our favourite series. Paul Temple and his female accomplice, Steve, solved innumerable crimes for the benefit of their avid listeners. Howard Marion Crawford, (yes, that name again), and Kim Peacock were well cast as successive Paul Temples, while Marjorie Westbury played Steve from the late Thirties onwards.

War time comedy radio is probably best remembered for such classics as 'ITMA' and 'Much Binding in the Marsh', but our young set acquired a taste, and a distinct preference, for variety programmes.

'Music Hall', which was broadcast on Saturday evenings, had a familiar pattern, and never failed to entertain at some point in its duration.

Frequent performers on Music Hall were 'Rawitz and Landauer on two pianos', and Ann Ziegler and Webster Booth, who emulated Jeanette MacDonald and Nelson Eddy, in close harmony duets. Peter Cavanagh provided impersonations of all the contemporary personalities of note, invariably signing-off by saying, "This is the voice of them all". His most famous routine was a one-man interpretation of all the characters in ITMA.

We revelled in the gentle comedy provided by Jeanne De Casalis, who played the feather-brained housewife, Mrs Feather, causing great confusion with her telephone conversations. 'Red Sails in the Sunset' introduced the comedienne Suzette Tarry, parading down to earth, everyday philosophy in her role as a BBC charlady.

We hardly ever missed the Sunday evening 'Happidrome' variety shows which were broadcast between 1941 and 1947. The infantile humour of Mr Lovejoy, Ramsbottom and Enoch, helped both young and old to cast the care of the austerity years to one side for just a little while. Enoch's catchphrase 'Let me tell you!' became a national slogan.

Apart from Charles Shadwell and the Variety Orchestra, the regular background musical accompaniment, as we performed our daily routines, was provided by such regulars as 'Big Bill Campbell and his Rocky Mountain Rhythm', 'Troise and his Mandoliers', and 'Felix Mendelssohn and his Hawaiian Serenaders'. 'Big Bill' would always make our day when he said, "Give us a song Panhandle!"

When the late King George VI gave his annual Christmas broadcast from Buckingham Palace, every single one of us willed him on, as he courageously fought against a speech impediment. None of us were cynical about the contents of his Christmas message; the only sentiments in evidence were genuine support and affection.

Chapter 13

FIRST TASTES

In those blessed days before television infiltrated itself into our living-rooms, reading occupied a high priority amongst our leisure time activities. The local public library provided the nucleus in which our reading tastes were nurtured. It is amusing to recall how our parents and their friends waited eagerly to read Margaret Mitchell's 'Gone with the Wind', and more discretely 'Forever Amber' by Kathleen Winsor. This book contained the most risqué form of literature of the day.

Enid Blyton and Richmal Crompton's William books were our number one favourites, closely followed by Percy F Westerman, and Captain W E Johns, as we approached our teens. The Chalet School stories of Elinor M Brent-Dyer, together with Barbara Euphan Todd's, 'Worzle Gummidge' books found favour with both boys and girls. Over forty years later it is somehow reassuring to note that several of these authors have retained their popularity with present day youngsters.

During the dark pre-Christmas afternoons we lived in magical anticipation of the one certain present we were sure to receive on Christmas morning, - the latest adventures of Rupert Bear. It is easy now to scoff at the innocent, rather moral stories with verse that we so eagerly looked forward to, but to us they possessed a real enchantment which never quite disappeared. Rupert's escapades with Bill Badger, Algy Pug, Edward Trunk and the Fox brothers, combined with the tranquil Nutwood setting wove a particular spell.

Bulking out many childrens' Christmas stockings during the Forties were the country stories of G Bramwell Evens, who we knew better as Romany of the BBC. The stories were simple, but factual accounts of such country denizens as Spook the Barn Owl, Pete and Prue the Partridges, and Hotchi the Hedgehog. Accompanied by pleasant line drawings and black and white photographs of Romany and his spaniel Raq, the adventures were read and re-read year after year.

However, to many of us the reading habit which became addictive during and just after the war, materialised with the circulation of the wide and diverse selection of weeklies known simply as 'Comics'.

The mere names of the first picture comics that we were introduced to, evoke nostalgic memories of many hours spent turning their 'War Economy' pages. Dandy and Beano; still available today; Knockout, Film Fun and Radio Fun all provided their own unlikely heros. The latest escapades of Desperate Dan, together with his cow pies, were as eagerly awaited as those of Lord Snooty and Keyhole Kate. Eggo the Ostrich and Korky the Cat were the stars of the colourful front pages of the Beano and Dandy; Christmas had really arrived when the title letters were bedecked with a liberal covering of snow.

But these amusing diversions were dwarfed into insignificance when we at last graduated to the high adventure found in the pages of the Wizard, Rover, Adventure, Hotspur and Champion. Their stories were anticipated, then devoured by us, week after week. Opinions and forecasts as to the possible course of events in future episodes were a daily source of conversation. If a poll had been taken to discover the most popular of all the characters whose adventures unfolded weekly in the small print comics, the chances are that most votes would have been cast for 'Wilson of the Wizard'. Wilson, a strange and lonely man, dressed in his one piece garment of home-spun yarn, had imbibed the mysterious elixir which had succeeded in slowing his heart-beat down to only two or three beats each minute. This enabled him to produce prodigious athletic feats. His first encounter with a steam engine portrayed him 'escaping' between the lines of the railway track with, of course, the train in noisy pursuit. It is scarcely necessary to add that Wilson won by a distance.

Another larger than life hero was H K Rodd whose 'hair was the colour of burnished gold'. He also possessed seemingly miraculous powers. In one never to be forgotten instalment H K Rodd was involved in providing a radio commentary on a football match. As the ball was played innocuously from defence by the home team, H K Rodd was heard to shout 'Goal!' into his microphone. A few more passes and perhaps a minute later, and sure enough a goal was scored. H K had wonderful powers of anticipation.

Baldy Hogan, football player-manager extra-ordinary, also had ingenious ways of enabling his team to be successful. Because a key member of his side was colour-blind, Baldy arranged for large circles to be designed on his players' stockings. This enabled the player with defective eye-sight to distinguish them from the usual stripes. Prior to this the colour-blind footballer had been guilty of passing the ball to members of the opposing team.

Rob Higson, cricketer, and Tuffy Tufton, footballer, were our other sporting favourites, while our number one private eye was 'Colwyn Dane, Tec', of the Champion. He solved innumerable baffling cases with great aplomb.

Swapping comics with friends and neighbours was done regularly and systematically and proved to be an exercise in sensible economics. A charming, tiny, middle-aged lady who lived nearby was a most enthusiastic dealer in this turnover of reading matter. Her small bright eyes and rosy complexion shone with enthusiasm as our transactions were concluded. Mint, glossy comics from our local newsagent cost tuppence each, but there was no difficulty in selling back numbers at half-price to school friends. Twelve comics sold at a penny each meant a night out in the cheapest stall seats at one of our local cinemas. It also encouraged the beginnings of business enterprise.

The style of English Language used in those comic narratives was far from outrageous, and there were relatively few spelling mistakes. Our English master positively encouraged this preliminary reading. There is no doubt that it was a useful precursor to what was to become a lifetimes' habit as our tastes gradually matured.

Chapter 14

OPEN ALL HOURS

My Aunt and Uncle lived just five miles away across the Leicestershire border in the small market and hosiery town of Hinckley. They had no children of their own and treated my brother and myself with affection and generosity all their lives. They owned a corner green-grocers shop long before supermarkets were dreamed of. It became a prosperous way of living, like countless other similar establishments which were to be found in virtually every other street during the Forties.

I visited them frequently; either cycling the five miles to Hinckley or catching the Midland Red bus for a fare of tuppence-halfpenny.

The approach to my Uncle's shop was made via a short-cut alongside the parish church, which lead to some rather flat and unimaginative ornamental gardens. Near the exit gates was a small railed enclosure holding a tree lined pond on which swans and a variety of wildfowl were always to be seen. During the winter of 1947 they made a pitiful sight, standing motionless and disconsolate on ice so thick it proved difficult to penetrate. I was always given fragments of bread with which to feed them on my return to the bus stop.

The shop itself was positioned in the front room of a large end terraced house and was a skilful demonstration in the efficient utilisation of every square inch of space. Each morning, before 7.00 am, vegetables and fruit would be placed lovingly in neat layers on wooden staging that had been erected on the pavement each side of the narrow shop door. Fresh cakes and bread arrived daily before the shop was open, and were distributed on glass shelves in the east facing window, to avoid the later heat of the day. The remainder of the small shop was an Aladdin's Cave mixture of provisions, ranging from buttons and thread to shoe polish, and from tomato sauce to porridge oats. Sugar, in large sacks was delivered wholesale to the shop and one of my first tasks as junior grocery assistant was to weigh it meticulously, a pound at a time, into dark blue strong paper bags.

Small queues of customers were ever-present during the war years, dwindling away in the late Fifties as the first supermarkets began to undercut the prices of corner shop grocers.

Taking 'points' from his customers' ration books was a particular irritation to my uncle, and on occasions I would help him to sort them into categories for his official returns. We performed this ritual in the evenings, after the shop had closed for the day, at his compact oak desk. Grocery orders were telephoned through to him from rather superior sounding clients; their requests being answered politely from Hinckley 210, even though lunch was often being partaken. Almost fifty years on, the highly polished work-worn desk has come to rest in my own small front hall.

For several years in the early Forties, I spent two weeks of the summer holidays acting as the official errand boy for the shop. To me, the most attractive part of the job was being permitted to use the sturdy, black, very upright cycle, on which I pursued the grocery round. It had a large wicker basket suspended from the handlebars, together with a black, metal plate crossbar, which informed everyone in Hinckley that W E Coles was 'THE' green grocer to visit.

I came to know the back streets of the town very well during those working holidays, and invariably received a friendly reception from the kindly Leicestershire folk.

In addition to being provided with superb home-cooked food, (my aunt had been in service at Sudeley Castle some years beforehand), I was given a crisp, new, one pound note at the end of the week as a reward for my most enjoyable employment.

The shop was open for business all day on Saturday, and also on Sunday mornings, but the Thursday half-day closing was sacrosanct, and adhered to religiously, as it provided the only opportunity in the week for an outing. On this longed-for afternoon we would travel in my uncle's immaculately polished, black Hillman Minx saloon, to visit his two spinster sisters who lived in Hamilton Street near the centre of Leicester. They kept an identical shop to their brother's, and the meeting proved a useful opportunity for them to compare experiences, prices and sundry other problems that arose from week to week.

I was the recipient of a gift, usually a book, on most of my visits to Leicester and was allowed to choose it myself from a cheerful bookseller's shop in the city centre. The first title I selected was, Sabatini's 'The Black Swan', a tale of pirates, which I found to be extremely tedious when attempting to read it in my small comfortable bedroom, set on the east side of the shop back in Hinckley. A more successful choice was, Westell's 'Let's watch the birds', which contained small black and white sketches of well known British birds, set in many pages of print. This rather unattractive book nevertheless helped to nurture my own lifelong interest in natural history. It was soon to be followed by the annual volumes of country life adventures involving Romany and Nomad of the BBC.

Once, for a special treat, during my working week at the shop, I was taken, together with my cousins, to a cinema in Hinckley where we saw Rex Harrison in 'Blithe Spirit'.

The evening was made even more enjoyable because our seats were positioned in the front row of the circle, rather than the initial eye-straining stalls that I was more accustomed to.

During the Nineteen Twenties my aunt and uncle had obtained positions in service at Merevale Hall, near Atherstone. In due course my aunt progressed to Sudeley Castle near Winchcombe, in the Cotswolds, where she became a housekeeper. Many years later I visited Sudeley Castle as a tourist and found the experience to be quite fascinating.

It was a hot, rather humid day in August when, together with perhaps thirty other tourists, I explored the impressive Castle and its attractive surrounding gardens. When I hesitantly mentioned to one of the senior guides that I was the nephew of a former housekeeper, her response was one of genuine interest, mingled together with a considerable amount of charm. I was whisked away from the well trodden tourist route, and secreted through a door marked 'Private', to the area of the Castle where the 'below stairs' staff had worked many years previously.

Connecting the ornate rooms to the servants quarters was, what can only be described as, an underground passage. My well informed guide graphically portrayed how my aunt, together with other members of the kitchen staff, would have carried, or wheeled on trolleys, food from the kitchen, and fuel from the outhouses, through the tunnel, before ascending the wooden staircase to the living quarters. Coal was carefully wrapped in newspapers to avoid soiling carpets and furniture.

My aunt and uncle married in the late Nineteen Twenties before moving to Hinckley where they commenced their grocery business. It was well established at the outbreak of war and flourished successfully until 1957. Their deserved prosperity was earned through long hours and consistently hard work. The cellar below the shop floor, (which served as an air-raid shelter from 1940 to 1942), had steep wooden steps used by my uncle on countless occasions during the day, as he shouldered heavy sacks and boxes of provisions to the shop above.

His vegetable produce was always of the highest quality, being obtained from celebrated local growers in the surrounding Leicestershire villages. He would purchase apples, pears, and plums from Sunday afternoon trips made along the Fosse Way to the Cotswolds. This was well before the 'pick your own' signs became widespread.

One aspect of his acquisition of superb examples of all types of fruit and vegetables invariably struck me as having a slightly dubious quality. My uncle regularly entered most of the local late-summer produce shows, exhibiting the pick of his collection. Just as regularly he swept the board, winning the majority of classes in direct opposition to the local allotment holders. He made no secret as to the source of his prize winning exhibits, and was truly elated when showing to us his officially awarded certificates. Obviously the rules and regulations, relating to the exhibition of fruit and vegetables at Hinckley shows contained a sizeable loophole which enabled my uncle to be the undisputed champion, while not actually possessing a garden or allotment.

Another aspect of corner shop life in the Nineteen Forties that appeared to work perfectly well was the co-operation between shop holders. Immediately across the quiet side road from my uncle's shop was a similar establishment selling many identical products, but with the addition of wines and spirits. The two shops pursued their trade in a perfectly amicable, and it must be said, profitable way, with both owners assisting each other when shortages of certain commodities arose.

Sitting with my uncle on Sunday mornings in Hinckley Parish Church, I was always given a half crown-piece to place on the collection plate. I experienced numerous fantasies during the course of the service, in which I found many more satisfactory ways of utilising the large silver coin which lay in my palm.

Whenever there was a national cause for celebration, but particularly on VE and VJ days, huge Union Jacks on stout flagpoles were thrust from all the upstairs windows of the shop.

In the late Nineteen Fifties, when the shop at Hinckley no longer proved to be a viable economic concern, my aunt and uncle bought a house at Weddington and remained there for the rest of their lives.

They share the same grave in Weddington Churchyard. It is positioned by the boundary fence to the left of the church entrance.

Chapter 15

CRICKETERS

When First Class Cricket resumed after the war years we had already acquired a sketchy knowledge of our more famous white-flannelled heroes. The BBC radio commentaries covering the Victory Test Matches brought to our attention the names of players who had themselves spent much of the previous six years far away from the playing arenas.

Lindsay Hassett, Keith Miller and Cecil Pepper, who were members of the 1945 Australian Services team, immediately became larger-than-life figures in our cricket-starved imaginations.

The resumption of the County Cricket programme in 1946 provided us with the opportunity of sampling the pleasures of First-Class Cricket for the first time in our brief span of years.

Residing on the County border we found it to be much more practical to travel to see the Leicestershire County Eleven, rather than take an LMS train to Birmingham and then wait patiently in a queue for a bus to Edgbaston. An additional advantage that our support of the Leicestershire team gave to us was that they occasionally played on small country grounds, well away from the city centre.

Our first live experience of top class cricket occurred when we made the short journey to the compact, picturesque ground at Barwell, where Leicestershire were competing against Warwickshire. As all the seating accommodation had long since disappeared when we arrived, we were allowed to stretch out full-length on the turf alongside the boundary line. Looking up at our heroes from this supine position produced the illusion of making them much taller than they actually were, and they became, consequently, even more god-like.

Warwickshire, who fielded first, were led by Peter Cranmer whose dapper, military bearing gave him an air of undisputed authority. The fact that he was not only a capable all-round cricketer but also a rugger international impressed us even more.

R H Maudsley and Richard Sale, although possibly considered to be relatively average players on the County circuit, patrolled the covers with such turf-consuming athleticism that from our worm's-eye view it was as if they had acquired superhuman speed and agility.

* * *

In the late Forties Leicestershire cricket revolved around a core of ever-present, hard-working players, who, while scarcely reaching the pinnacle of cricketing fame, nevertheless managed to provide a considerable amount of entertainment for their avid teenage followers.

On numerous occasions we witnessed Gerry Lester and the Australian Vic Jackson, bowl their medium-pace and offbreak deliveries over after over in attempts to break developing stands. Jack Walsh, another Australian, bowled his looping left-arm spinners for what seemed to be interminable spells. While he was invariably the recipient of severe punishment from the opposing batsmen he still managed to reap an impressive harvest of wickets. Jack's analysis frequently seemed to read 5 for 95!

The Leicestershire wicket-keeper was Paddy Corrall, a diminutive figure almost completely enveloped by huge pads, his head surmounted by a baggy, fox-crested green cap. Although he was to sustain a serious injury from a flailing cricket bat, Paddy still managed to stump 187 victims and catch 381 more during his twenty year career.

Tall, imperious, and rather portly, Les Berry the Leicestershire captain regularly opened the innings for the County. He created an atmosphere of calm authority, and such was his dependability that he achieved 1000 runs eighteen times in twenty-five years.

While Les Berry was a mature and effective cricketer, our favourite player in the post-war team was Maurice Tompkin. He was not only a polished middle-order batsman, but with his shining halo of almost golden hair, and his fleetness of foot, he graced the cover-point position with the alertness of a gazelle. Our hero Maurice Tompkin scored 1000 runs in ten of the seasons he played. He died tragically in 1956 after an operation when he was just thirty-seven years of age.

Frequent visits to Grace Road gave us the privilege of seeing some of the finest batsmen in the land, even if they were usually members of the opposing team. A Len Hutton century was, in our youthful experience, the most majestic and technically correct innings we were ever to witness. One of Hutton's fellow Yorkshiremen, Gerald Smithson, widely regarded as the most promising batsmen of the day, impressed us also. Ironically enough he transferred to the Leicestershire Eleven in 1951.

Arguably one of the finest innings ever to be seen at Grace Road occurred in the summer holidays of 1948. Several of our school First Eleven caught a Midland Red Bus to Leicester on a fine August day to watch play in the Leicestershire versus Surrey County Championship match. On that day Laurie Fishlock, the Surrey left-handed batsman, repeatedly drove the ball over the boundary line to eventually reach 253, his highest-ever score.

A young lady sitting immediately in front of us sustained an egg-sized bruise when a vicious Fishlock cover-drive was halted by her leg, leaving her hopping in anguish, completely ruining her day.

In the halcyon summer of 1947 a coachload of very excited teenagers travelled to Trent Bridge to see England in Test Match combat against the South Africans. Owing to the size of the crowd we were permitted to encroach onto the grass just outside the boundary chalk-line, exactly as we had done at Barwell during the previous season.

The sight of Len Hutton's stumps being uprooted by the Springbok's young fast bowler Lindsay Tuckett was relived by us for months afterwards. Less exciting, but important from England's point of view, was the match-saving innings played by Norman Yardley.

While the day itself remained intensely memorable if only because it was our first experience of Test Cricket, it was rather remarkable that on the return coach journey the main talking point revolved around the slightly built South African cover-point, Terence Harris. He had given a superb demonstration of fielding, swooping repeatedly on the ball just in front of our reclining ranks. We were never to forget that marvellous exhibition, and it came as no surprise to discover that he was, in fact, a noted rugby fly-half, having represented his country in that position.

Denis Compton and Bill Edrich, whose year it was, did not, that day anyway, remain long in our memories.

Chapter 16

SIGNAL LEYS GORSE

Signal Leys Gorse lies between Weddington and Caldecote in the form of a narrow L-shaped strip of woodland, which follows the banks of the River Anker for almost half a mile. Its rich variety of trees include Scots pine, oak, beech, lime, horse-chestnut, sycamore and many tall ash trees. The wood comes to life each April when Norway maples burst into pale yellow blossom at regular intervals along its southern face. Elder bushes show masses of creamy flowers in June and a medium sized holly tree is consistent each autumn with its small clusters of berries. Alders dip their roots into the river the whole extent of the wood.

Situated nearly one mile to the north of Weddington Church, it seemed that Signal Leys was the point we invariably aimed for in our country excursions, even though we did not consciously plan to do so.

Celandines appeared amongst the soft soil on the sheltered river banks as early as mid-January in mild winters, their burnished yellow providing the first hint of Spring. On either side of the narrow footpaths clumps of bluebells and wood anemones were to be found, while delicate wood sorrel and wild arum, or cuckoo pint, made their appearance early in April. From May onwards red campion and cow parsley provided a colourful contrast as they gradually covered the well worn tracks.

It was here that we began to discover our interest in observing birds, a way of life that remained with us as childhood gradually receded. With the cheapest and most inefficient binoculars, combined with infinite patience, we were able to record the resident birds that, at the time, we assumed to be great rarities. A fresh species added to our list provoked great excitement when first spotted then verified against our battered copy of the 'Observers Book of Birds'.

Weddington Church

A Treecreeper was a permanent resident in Signal Leys, unobtrusively ascending the undersides of branches high in the alders, paying little attention to the young bird-watchers below, who were never able to discover its nesting site.

Each November olive-hued Siskins from Eastern Europe performed as acrobatically as Blue Tits; feeding from the small coal-black cones growing prolifically on the gnarled branches of the alders.

Almost hidden by the emerging branches of a Scots pine a Tawny Owl slept the day away; pellets containing the bones of voles and shrews lying on the surface of the wood beneath him.

At irregular intervals we heard the high pitched whistle of a turquoise and blue Kingfisher, and marvelled at the arrow-like flight as it sped around the bends of the sluggish, slow flowing river. On one occasion we were fortunate enough to see a Kingfisher dive into the water from the muddy river bank and emerge with a minnow in its dagger-like beak.

In the extreme winter of 1947 we were to record our only comparative rarity. Busily extracting seeds from pine cones a small party of tawny and olive Crossbills allowed us an extended observation period before flying from the gorse. We were never to see Crossbills again at Caldecote.

Willow Warblers, slim and restless, nested in the dense brambles along Signal Leys Lane. Here also the brief exuberant song flight of Whitethroats was heard as they leapt from the hedgerows every ten yards or so. Willow tits, and secretive, tiny Goldcrests appeared from time to time, as did salmon-breasted, black-capped Bullfinches piping mournfully as they flew undulatingly from the early blossom.

We ate the first tender leaf buds from the hawthorns, relishing the fresh, nutty taste. We called this repast 'Bread and Cheese'.

In early Spring the fields surrounding Signal Leys Gorse were host to hovering Skylarks, their song providing a constant melodic background as we passed by. The sentinel horse-chestnut tree at the entrance to the Gorse allowed vantage points for Chaffinches to repeat their cheerful throat-swelling flourish.

As March progressed, Chiffchaffs, the first returning migrants, lisped their two-syllable call from a hazel copse just beyond the wood. These sleek warblers were so trusting that they sang unconcernedly only a few feet above our heads, disturbing pollen from catkins which settled gently on the drifts of wood anemones always to be found there.

A shallow diamond-glinting, stone-bedded stream ran through the heart of the Chiffchaff copse. The low willow and elder growth surrounding it was so profuse that it kept the stream successfully hidden from most visitors to its pleasant environs.

Here on the stream's banks, reclining as if asleep, we found a dead Vixen, perfect in every detail, her eyes still bright and moist.

One late August evening we disturbed a Sandpiper from the muddy fringe of the River Anker which meandered alongside the length of Signal Leys. The cream and brown wader was sufficiently unusual for us to pursue it along the river bank where it flirted and bobbed before flying low to the water's edge some distance away.

This occasional visitor to Caldecote was followed late in November by another newcomer to the area. A fine chestnut-coloured Woodcock remained motionless for a second or two before whirring away from the tender green shoots of a spring barley field which lay close to Signal Leys Lane. Long beak pointing earthwards, he sped low across the field to the Anker Cottage gardens with us trailing in his wake, soon to be disappointed when we were unable to locate him again.

Both the Sandpiper and Woodcock were isolated sightings. Sadly we were never to see them again at Caldecote.

In high summer the Southern face of Signal Leys was witness to a remarkable gathering of sickle-winged Swifts. They flickered up and down the length of the wood, the click of their mandibles audible as they snapped-up the myriad insects so abundant aloft on the humid summer air. We were able to see in detail their sooty-brown plumage and lighter throat patch as they hastened past us at shoulder-height, disdainfully indifferent to our presence.

The Swifts' impressive performance was admired by us for many years, and even now, several decades later, the sheltered wood-face still attracts small numbers of them.

Each year, in early June, we would be on the look-out for the first Orange-tip butterflies patrolling the lane, enforcing their territorial rights. These were followed in August by Speckled Woods performing the same ritual. Meadow Browns, undoubtedly the commonest butterfly that we pursued in our boyhood, were soon joined by Peacocks, Small Tortoiseshells and Red Admirals. They were always to be found first of all flying above, then settling on the seeding, pungent hogweed that arose six feet high on either side of the Lane. We cut sections from the dried hollow stems of the hogweed using them as ready-made pea-shooters. Waxen-red hawthorn berries became our ammunition, as we held a supply of several berries in our mouths before skilfully manipulating one with our tongues to the tube entrance. Although hawthorn berries were occasionally swallowed and lodged in nostrils we suffered no permanent after-effects; the pea-shooters remaining accurate, if irritating weapons.

Gradually summer mellowed into Autumn and as we walked through the Lane, superb Emperor Dragonflies, their green and turquoise abdomens intersected by black stripes, would fly aggressively past us at head height. They frequently settled on hogweed and bramble, luxuriating in the pleasant warmth, their gauze wings shimmering in the sun's rays which penetrated obliquely through the overhanging branches.

When misty October arrived we walked through the same lane, holding between thumb and index finger a twig bent into the shape of a small bow. With this simple device we collected hundreds of dew-bedecked spiders' webs that had become visible on the dripping hedgerows. Soon we had gathered a mesh of translucent, silk-like material that stretched unbroken in the arc of the bent twig. It reflected the sunlight, and delighted us by giving glimpses of other colours in the spectrum.